Praise for Th

"This book will transform lives. Through her ~~~~ and witness, Chaena teaches you how to heal...for real... and begin living a purpose-filled life. I'll definitely be sharing the message of healing *intentionally* with my clients and my colleagues."

-Dr. Asha, Creator of Healthy Conversations and Founder, The Temple Fit Company

"The *Value in Violation* reminds us that the very thing that broke us can be the thing that builds us. With a powerful step-by-step framework, Chaena teaches us how to go from a place of pain to a place of purpose."

-Kary Oberbrunner, author of *Elixir Project*, *Your Secret Name*, and *The Deeper Path*

"This book tackles the topics of trauma, betrayal and violation head on and challenges us to shift our perspective on their true value. Whether your violation is domestic violence, abandonment or infidelity by your spouse, or sexual assault by someone you thought you could trust, Chaena shows you how to find the beauty in the betrayal one purposeful step at a time."

-Dr. Regina Spellmon, Founder of Get Briefed and author of *From Pieces to Peace*

"With the #MeToo movement making waves the world over, society is just now starting to acknowledge what up until now has been a painful, guilty secret for far too many people. If you have been violated in any way by someone you trusted, whether it be physically, emotionally or spiritually, you owe it to yourself to read Chaena Hollist's book. It is a true life-changer and will help guide you out of the darkness and into the light."

-Deb Kastner, Publishers Weekly Bestselling Author

The Value in Violation

Discover How to Heal Intentionally, Turn Your Pain into Purpose, and Find Beauty After Betrayal

CHAENA HOLLIST

AUTHOR ACADEMY elite

Printed in the United States of America

Published by Author Academy Elite
P.O. Box 43, Powell, OH 43035
www.AuthorAcademyElite.com

Cover design by Virtually Possible Designs

All Scripture quotations are taken from The Holy Bible, *New International Version® NIV®*. Copyright © 1973, 1978, 1984, 2011 by Biblica, Inc.™ Used by permission. All rights reserved worldwide.

Disclaimer: The content in this book is intended for educational and informational purposes only and not as a substitute for medical or mental health care. It is meant to be a supplement and guide. The author and publisher will not be liable for any physical, emotional, or psychological damages including, but not limited to, special, incidental, consequential, or other damages. Readers should regularly consult a medical professional in matters relating to his/her health and particularly with respect to any symptoms that may require diagnosis or medical attention.

This book contains stories in which the author has changed people's names and some of their personal details in order to protect their privacy. Any perceived slights of specific persons, peoples, or organizations are unintentional. While all attempts have been made to ensure the accuracy of information provided in this publication, the Author and Publisher assumes no responsibility for errors, omissions, or contrary interpretations of the subject matter therein.

Library of Congress Control Number: 2018958188
Paperback ISBN- 978-1-64085-453-6
Hardcover ISBN- 978-1-64085-454-3
Ebook ISBN- 978-1-64085-455-0

Table of Contents

Part One: Intervention

Part Two: Treatment

Treatment: Phase One: Recovery

Treatment: Phase Two: Re-Assessment

Treatment: Phase Three: Rehabilitation

Part Three: Discharge

Informed Consent

Some of the topics discussed in this book as well as experiences of my life may bring up some intense emotions as you read about them. It may be because you've experienced your own relationship wound(s) and that's the reason you even picked up this book. On the other hand it may be because you know someone who has or work with people who have. If while reading you begin to feel overwhelmed, remember to acknowledge and honor any feelings that rise up.

I'm beyond humbled that you've decided to set aside some of your valuable time to read this book. I honor you because although you may have experienced pain or disappointment in your past, you also know you are still worthy of what you desire.

By agreeing to read this book you are consenting to walking alongside me on a journey full of hard truths, a life-changing process, and inspiring insight about being healed and staying whole.

INTRODUCTION

Acknowledge Your Wound

It was September 23rd, 1999, and I was sitting in the living room feeling like an absolute shell of my former self. Three days before I had turned thirteen years old. I was sitting in a room I'd inhabited every day watching TV and playing with my siblings. But in that moment, my home felt unsafe... even foreign.

Why? I was in a hospital gown. But it wasn't just *what* I was wearing, but *why* I was wearing it. I'd had to give a nurse all of my clothes. They needed them for the police investigation. See, my dad's best friend, Lamont, had broken into our home at around three o'clock that morning and raped me in the bed I shared with my little sister.

Now I knew why last week he'd asked my dad, who was an over-the-road truck driver, when he would next be going on the road. It was so he would know the best time to make his move. He'd also managed to enter our home without forced entry, from what the police said. They told us he must have stolen a key or knew how to break into our home quietly, since he'd been in our home many times before. Then to top it off, driven by an audacity I will never understand, he assaulted me as my ten-year-old sister lay in the same queen-size bed we shared. He simply squeezed in between the two of us and seemed to dare either of us to move.

And I didn't. I froze. I laid still while he assaulted me. My main concern was for my sister. I felt like if I made a scene or screamed, she couldn't pretend to be asleep anymore. Then he might have hurt her, too. So I froze, closed my eyes, and silently begged for it to end.

After he finished assaulting me, he left for a few seconds and then came back to the foot of my bed. He knelt down and offered me money to "keep quiet." It was only after this that I found my voice. It had felt as if I had swallowed cotton and couldn't speak during the entire time he was assaulting me, but in that moment I reclaimed my voice. I didn't know how he would respond. Would he hurt me? Would he kill me? I didn't know. But I also couldn't let my fear keep me silent for a moment longer. It had something to do with him trying to buy my silence after he had just stolen my innocence. I yelled, "No! Leave me alone!"

He seemed shocked that I had actually spoken out loud and he hurried out the door to make sure no one else in my family woke up and saw him. I was proud of myself for yelling at him but conflicted about whether I should have done so sooner. My norm had always been to freeze when confronted with something I deemed as stressful or dangerous. He knew this about me. That's probably why he chose to violate me. In his mind I was the *perfect victim*.

At that moment, sitting on the couch in my hospital gown, I felt completely confused. I couldn't comprehend what had just happened to me. I also had no idea what it meant. I had actually just gotten saved at church a couple of months prior. The night I got saved the preacher told me that because I was saved, "I had been bought with a price and Jesus had paid it all." I remember thinking at the time, "Well if I'm worth so much, why did God let this happen to me? And since this happened to me, what does this mean for how much I'm worth *now*?"

I didn't know the answer to that question. But I knew I felt exposed. I felt scared. And I felt...betrayed.

So there I was, sitting on my living room couch, fresh from the hospital and feeling the slight draft on my back from my open hospital gown. It was barely held together by two flimsy little straps. I remember lying to my little brothers about the reason I couldn't go to school that day. I just couldn't bring myself to tell them what had happened. So I just sat there, too frozen to cry, too tired to think straight and too traumatized to go back into my own room and change out of that stupid gown.

That was *my* first significant relationship wound. Someone I knew and trusted had violated, hurt and betrayed me. A couple of years after that incident Lamont stood trial and was found 'Not Guilty' in a court of law for what he had done to me. The violation I experienced was disregarded by the legal system and I was left to find my own peace with the outcome. I had to move on. It was hard, but I did. I excelled in high school, both academically and athletically. I was active in my church and in my community. I somehow managed to push Lamont and that whole incident to the back corners of my mind. But little did I know how much this wound and how it "healed" (or didn't) would continue to impact my life for many years to come.

At our very core, human beings are relational. We were created this way. So it goes without saying that when we suffer a wound within relationship, the impact can be devastating.

Just like with physical wounds, some relationship wounds are surface-level and require just a band-aid and a little time to heal. This might be the petty argument with a family member or the no-hard-feelings break-up with someone you dated for a couple of months. But then there are some relationship wounds which after they happen leave you broken and empty. They turn your life upside down and you, in a sense, have to learn how to walk all over again. Sticking with the wound analogy, these wounds cut deep and sometimes we can't even see the extent of the *internal* damage done. If left to heal on their own, they can lead to an infection that keeps affecting and infecting our relationships and our lives for many years to come.

This doesn't have to be you though. You've managed to get your hands on a book that will show you how to be proactive and intentional about your healing process. You don't just have to *hope* that you can move past the person who hurt you, *hope* you can get your self-esteem back, or *hope* you'll have the healthy and thriving relationships you deserve.

Now you can *expect* to.

What type of relationship wound or wounds have you experienced? Were they from emotional, physical or verbal abuse by someone you loved? Or were they the result of infidelity, psychological abuse or abandonment by your spouse or partner? It's important to note that relationship wounds aren't only those committed by an intimate partner. Relationship wounds involving molestation, acquaintance rape, sexual assault, sexual harassment and spiritual abuse are some of the most painful events a human being can experience.

All of these wounds are *violations*— or acts that are without consent, disturbing, and offensive. They're complex and their impact can cripple. I know this firsthand as I've experienced many of these violations in my own life. However, there came a time when I could no longer afford to keep putting band-aids on wounds that needed surgery and rehab. I had to be intentional and deliberate if I wanted to be whole and one day have a healthy marriage and fulfilling relationships. I chose to be intentional about stopping the cycle of toxic relationships and started creating the healthy relationships I wanted. I couldn't afford to stay broken. It had cost me too much.

So now I ask you…

Do you want to take control of your life and no longer be held hostage by the hurt you've endured at the hands of someone you trusted?

Would you like to know the blueprint, the discharge instructions and a practical step-by-step process to heal that hurt so you can manifest and maintain the relationships you deserve?

If so, I wrote this book especially for you. I know what it feels like to live in the fog of betrayal, to wear my pain on my sleeve (and not even know it) and to struggle in the area of relationships because I'm experiencing them and seeing them through the lens of my wounds.

But I also know the process I eventually went through to *intentionally* heal and manifest an amazing marriage that has produced two beautiful children. I've witnessed hundreds of people in my time as a social worker overcome devastating relationship wounds. While working with them, I paid close attention to the stages and phases they went through. Some of them went through each and every phase and their journey was inspiring to witness. I also saw many who stopped halfway through the healing process or unknowingly skipped important steps.

A few years ago I noticed one question being asked repeatedly by clients in my work at a shelter for family violence victims. They would ask, "I know that there's a process of healing after brokenness, but what are the exact steps in that process so I can make sure I do it right?" Eventually, I had to sit down and start writing, because I'd learned the answer through my own life experiences and in my work with others. To be clear, I didn't create the phases of the process, nor did I carry myself through them. However, lessons gleaned from my own experiences, evidence gathered from numerous academic studies on the subject, as well as insight gained from God and scripture, helped me develop a framework for recovering from brokenness and betrayal. I created the **Heal Intentionally Blueprint©** and began coaching others through the process of overcoming offense, turning their pain into purpose and finding beauty after betrayal. I've seen the powerful impact it has had on my clients and now I'm going to share it with you, my beloved reader.

Healing doesn't simply happen by luck, chance or because enough time passes. It requires intention and purposeful action.

I applaud you for taking action.

PART ONE

Intervention

CHAPTER ONE

Stop Your Bleeding

Have you ever watched a movie or television show where your favorite character gets shot? I think we all have. Your heart drops and you might think, "Oh my gosh…No!" Sometimes I'm so into it I even start yelling at the TV screen and talking to the other characters. You don't have to admit to it like I'm about to but I've been known to get glued to a good TV show and binge-watch for hours. I like all types of genres but I've watched my fair share of crime and medical dramas. They're probably my two favorite. One of the things you learn once you've watched just a few of those shows is there are so many different things one can focus on when someone's been shot. It's usually a chaotic and scary scene. People are forced to decide whether to focus on the victim, the shooter or themselves. If someone is shot, they might worry about whether they're going to make it, whether any internal organs were hit, whether there's an exit wound and even what the long-term impact of the wound will be.

All of these are valid concerns, but the most important thing to do in that moment is to STOP THE BLEEDING.

The biggest threat at that very moment is the possibility that the victim could lose too much of the life-sustaining blood pumping through her veins. Fail to apply enough pressure to the wound, even if it's painful, and she could die. Yes, she's mad at the person who wounded her and yes, she worries about whether she's going to make it through this thing, but in order to get "justice" or live to see what lies ahead, it's critical to put all effort into stopping the damage and stopping the bleeding.

Well in this book, we're dealing with wounds...relationship wounds...and we are committing to stopping the bleeding.

A relationship wound can be devastating. I define a relationship wound as *an injury, whether emotional, psychological, physical or spiritual that is inflicted by someone you know, like (even love) and trust.* Being violated by someone you know and trust is one of the most painful experiences humans encounter. These wounds can cut deep...really deep, even penetrating the body, spirit and soul of a person.

Relationship wounds are so much more common than they should be. We human beings can be brutal to one another. Yet so many of us don't take recovering from relationship wounds as seriously as we ought to because many times there's no blood to see or an actual wound to treat. The truth is, we don't have to be superwoman (or superman), although many of us have been auditioning for the role our entire lives. Bullets don't just bounce off of us. What's happened is that many people are walking around with the bullets still lodged in them. They were hit, but they kept going. They kept pushing. Too many people have been wounded but have continued living life without addressing or removing the bullets they've been hit by along the way.

The person(s) who harmed you may not have been concerned about your feelings, but I invite you to honor yourself by acknowledging your wound(s). Dealing directly with your pain will help you determine and reach your purpose. I also invite you to acknowledge that you may still be bleeding, even if it has been years since that incident or relationship. If you're willing to accept my invitation to take this journey of truly exploring, seeing and falling in love with yourself and your story in a deeper and more meaningful way, that means you're willing to do the "work." Doing the *work* is what stops the bleeding, or the cycle of brokenness and disappointment. Doing the work puts a shield of protection around you and helps you avoid staying in unhealthy relationships or toxic environments a second longer than necessary in the future. Doing the *work* will help you go from feeling wounded and damaged to remembering your value cannot be stolen, and that it is something you were born with.

You're too valuable to live your life walking around with unresolved wounds. Living with an unresolved relationship wound is the equivalent of being on a battlefield with a preexisting injury, no weapon and no protective gear.

It leaves you vulnerable and likely to be hurt again.

> *Living with an unresolved relationship wound is the equivalent of being on a battlefield with a preexisting injury, no weapon and no protective gear.*

This is because relationship wounds don't tend to be one-offs. They tend to happen again and again if they don't heal completely, just like an infection that hasn't been properly treated will keep coming back. Wounds also tend to compound on one another. Some people experienced their first bad relationship wound as a child, some as a teenager and some as a young adult. But so many people barely deal with it, if at all, and invite the cycle of unhealthy, mediocre, or un-fulfilling relationships to continue. See, unfortunately, many people don't have the knowledge, tools or means to work with a qualified therapist or coach who might help them do the work they need to do to heal intentionally. So when people get hurt, they attach meaning to that person or experience (whatever helps them get through the day and sleep at night), they wait for the pain to subside and then move on in their lives. They numb their pain but they don't always stop the bleeding. Therefore, future relationship decisions are still driven by the memories, disappointments and drama of their past experiences.

The truth is that simply numbing your pain doesn't prevent you from being hurt again—quite the opposite. When you don't completely heal from a relationship wound, avoiding future pain becomes the driving force in your life, rather than inviting the vulnerability needed to have healthy relationships. Also, whenever fear has a front seat in your life, toxic people are drawn to you like sharks are drawn to the scent of blood. They can sense you are wounded and although you may feel fine and think you have it all together, there's blood in the water and they can smell it.

These sharks drift into your space and circle around your life in the form of new "baes", friends and even mentors. But if you have relationship wounds that you haven't dealt with you risk being re-victimized.[1] Until you stop the bleeding and truly heal intentionally, toxic, mediocre and unhealthy men and women will continue to be drawn to you like a shark is drawn to a wounded fish.

That puts a whole new meaning to the saying, "there's plenty of fish in the sea," doesn't it?

However, once you decide to heal intentionally, you stop that cycle. You'll find yourself remembering your value despite the violation. You'll learn how to honor your wounds without wearing them. Most of all, your new level of self-love will inevitably create an atmosphere where you can manifest the relationships you want and deserve while quickly repelling any that would bring you harm.

I take it from the fact that you're reading this book that you have already committed to stopping the bleeding. You're ready to undergo and learn this process of healing intentionally so that you can stop smelling like what you went through. You desire to repossess your own personal power and fall in love with yourself in a deeper way. You want to create or sustain healthy and mutually-beneficial relationships. Seeing the importance of this process is the first step. You're on your way.

The process of *healing intentionally* is like undergoing a medical procedure. You're not sick, but you've been wounded. Any medical procedure or treatment involves risks. In the next chapter, I'll make sure you know what those risks are so you go into this with your eyes wide open.

CHAPTER TWO

Understand Your Risks

Anything with a reward requires some degree of risk. There is no way of knowing exactly what the future holds, but you can get to a point where staying where you are is no longer acceptable to you. Continuing with the status quo won't cut it anymore. And even though you know it may get worse before it gets better, you're willing to risk short-term discomfort for long-term peace.

Have you ever had a bad toothache? If not, I don't wish one on you. It's absolutely terrible. The only comparable pain I've experienced is a labor contraction. Tooth pain can be dulled with medication but after a few hours it may come back with a vengeance. I remember coming home with my son right after giving birth. After being in the hospital, getting poked and prodded on and being in pain for days, I returned home and woke up from a short nap with sharp pains in my bottom jaw. It got bad so fast that a few hours later I was on the phone with a dentist's office, setting an appointment and asking for an extraction myself.

Did I feel like going into yet another medical office and being poked and prodded on some more? Absolutely not. Did I want to leave my breastfed five-day-old for even one moment? No, not at all. But I knew I wasn't going to be able to be present for my newborn if I was preoccupied with my pain. I also knew if I didn't undergo the extraction process there was a risk that an infection could develop and quickly spread to other parts of my body. I had just had c-section surgery and my immune system was a little busy figuring out what my body had gone through while giving birth. I was sure it didn't have the time or energy to deal with a festering tooth infection on top of that.

When I got to the dentist's office, the staff had me sign an informed consent document confirming I had read and understood the risks of the procedure. Just like with any medical procedure, there were risks involved in getting a tooth extracted. However, the biggest risk to my well-being was to continue to treat the symptoms with pain medications and wait it out, hoping the pain would go away on its own. And boy, did I have some good medications on hand, considering I had just had a c-section!

When you've been wounded in relationship, the wound is just as bad if not worse than a physical wound. There is damage done to your heart, your mind, your spirit, your self-esteem, your sense of safety and so many other aspects of you. It's a complex and complicated injury. The symptoms can ripple into our everyday lives and affect how we interact with the world around us.

Sometimes the pain of being hurt, violated and mistreated by someone is so deep that even after you "escape" it, just thinking about it can cause crippling emotional pain. So in order to move on with life, some people stuff, smother or ignore anything which could trigger a memory about that situation. On the other hand, others talk to anyone and everyone about all their drama in a superficial and face-saving way, but are scared to truly admit how much they're hurting on the inside. The truth is sometimes it's a little easier to air all our dirty laundry on social media and blast the person who hurt us than it is to truly grieve our losses and deal with our pain in an authentic way.

Then there are those who use distraction or re-direction to deal. They pack their days with so many things to do and places to be that there is not even time to think. Honestly, it can be an effective way to ignore our own mess. Been there, done that.

And of course, there's getting to know someone new so there's always someone in the room, on the other end of the line or responding to our text messages to save us from being alone and to help us avoid that annoyingly awkward silence.

The truth is, silence allows us to be alone with our thoughts and deal with ourselves and our stuff in a meaningful way. Silence is where it's quiet enough to hear God's still, small voice. It's quiet enough to hear our *own* voice. When there is silence and solitude there's no one and nothing there to distract us from the pain we may be feeling. Avoiding that silence ends up postponing our healing. At certain points of the healing process, pain has to quietly walk alongside us on our journey back to a place of wholeness. When we ignore the pain, it only gets louder and louder. When we listen to our

> *At certain points of the healing process, pain has to quietly walk alongside us on our journey back to a place of wholeness.*

pain in an intentional way, we can learn from it, we can address it and then we can heal it.

So there are risks to doing the work of healing intentionally. You risk being quiet, being present with yourself, being raw with your emotions and actually letting yourself feel whatever you need to feel…the anger, grief, apathy, sadness, despair and yes, the pain. Pain is never pleasant, but part of healing intentionally is giving your pain a purpose. For example, think about the pain that comes after you start running or lifting weights when you haven't worked out in a while. Yes, it hurts, but it's a necessary part of the process of becoming healthier and stronger.

Throughout this book I'll use some medical terms and concepts to remind you that the process of healing from relationship wounds is just like undergoing treatment for any other type of wound. There are risks involved. However, the worst pain is not the temporary and purposeful pain that comes with truly healing. It's the pain that will go away for a while, only to keep showing up uninvited and unwanted in your life.

So just to make sure you're "eyes wide open" on the risks and the benefits of going on this journey of *Healing Intentionally*, I'd like to share what will happen if you make the decision to stay where you are. You will limit yourself in three key areas:

Limit Your Living

Your wounds have a way of affecting you in a deeper way than almost anything else you experience in life. Even when we don't think about them every day or have managed to push them to the back corners of our minds, our souls still know. If you have an unresolved wound, you're living fractured and at half-capacity. Whether it's limiting your capacity for healthy and fulfilling relationships, physical well-being, financial blessings or spiritual maturity…failing to heal intentionally limits what's possible for your life. That's not because you don't deserve an abundant life. Instead, it's because unresolved wounds have a way of making you question your ability to create the life you deserve.

Limit Your Learning

There are very few positive things that can come from being hurt, but one for certain is the chance to learn and grow from it. Two of my favorite sayings are, "Experience is the best teacher," and, "Those who don't learn from their past are bound to repeat it." These are definitely true when it comes to being involved in a toxic or unhealthy relationship. If you do not fully heal, there is a chance that you'll find yourself in the same type of relationship or "situation-ship" again in the future.

The reality is, when you go through painful experiences, your brain will always try to make sense of it, regardless of how insensible it is. This is simple human biology. It will assign that person, those people, or that event a belief or many beliefs and file them into your memory. Then as you go through life, whenever something happens related to that experience, you will see it through pathways already created in your brain. One of the benefits to healing *well* is you'll create healthy and rational pathways instead of pathways built out of fear and trauma.

When you don't heal intentionally and give your heart and mind the best chance to recover, you limit your ability to learn and grow into the best version of yourself.

Limit Your Legacy

Your legacy is *the way and degree to which our lives impact the lives of those connected to us.* The futures of your children,

13

family members and others who are closely connected to you are impacted by how you live your life. Financial success can mean you are able to leave an inheritance for your family because ... legacy. Attending an Ivy League college could mean your child gets into Harvard or Yale without necessarily having the highest grades and test scores because ... legacy. Being a great artist could mean your children have a natural knack for creative work because ... legacy.

However, there is no way to make sure only the positive aspects of your life become your legacy. Legacy does not discriminate. Bad habits, hang ups, emotional issues, dysfunctional relationship skills and poor decision-making can just as effectively attach to those you're connected to, whether it be close friends, extended family or your children. Children especially will watch you like a hawk. They watch how you handle hurt, disappointment and difficulty. They watch how you deal with toxic people or toxic situations. They watch where you run to when you're wounded. But more importantly, many times they don't just watch. They also learn and imitate.

When you are deeply hurt or violated by someone or experience a relationship trauma like a divorce or bad breakup, those you love have to watch you go through the aftermath of it all. They get to watch you pick up the pieces. Many times they're empathetic and hurt because you hurt. But if you're haphazard about your healing process, you risk teaching your loved ones to do the same when they experience it. The bottom line is if you don't heal intentionally, you not only limit yourself, you limit those connected to you.

A doctor tells you about the risks to inform you about the stakes involved should you choose to stay where you are. I'm not a doctor, but my goal here is the same. The stakes are high. This is the quality of your life and relationships we are talking about here. Bear in mind, I'm not just talking about relationships with other people. Remember, when we're hurt by someone, our relationship with ourselves tends to get the biggest brunt of the impact. Our self-esteem, self-confidence and sense of self-worth endure real damage due to the guilt and shame that comes from being hurt by someone we trusted.

So yes, the stakes are high, but I want you to know you are right where you need to be. You deserve to feel worthy. You deserve to be whole so the only types of relationships you attract are with other *whole* people. You deserve to get to a place where you not only know you are fearfully and wonderfully-made, but you feel fearfully and wonderfully-made, and those whom you allow to be in relationship with you in the future will treat you as such.

Special Note to the Reader

The next section of the book, Part Two, dives into the *8 Steps of the Journey* necessary to heal after hurt and betrayal. I've called the next section TREATMENT because, like any treatment, it's a transformational process. It's a journey I've been on myself as a survivor. It's a journey I've helped other people take, as well. TREATMENT is divided into three phases: Recovery, Reassessment and Rehabilitation. Each *phase* contains critical *steps* everyone who experiences a wound by someone they trusted should take in order to turn that pain into purpose. The universal truths that are the basis of the steps in the *Heal Intentionally Blueprint©* are found in countless evidence-based medical and psychological journals, in the life of the world's most well-known historical figure, Jesus Christ, when He was betrayed and began a famous journey toward His purpose, as well as in the personal stories of men and women all over the world. These truths don't just apply to certain people or to certain worldviews. These truths will work for anyone who applies them.

My desire in writing this book is to outline these universal truths in a step-by-step way you can effectively apply to your own life so you can heal on purpose. In order to do this, I'll candidly share the wisdom I've gained throughout my career in the mental health field which *informed* the **Heal Intentionally Blueprint©**. I'll also share the insight I've gained from a few key scriptures that *inspired* the **Heal Intentionally Blueprint©**.

But as the saying goes, "Experience is the best teacher." So in this book, I'll also open up about my *own* experience of healing after violation, brokenness and betrayal. As I go through each of the eight steps, I'll invite you to *Peek into The Process*, where I'll share snapshots of my healing journey. I decided to share them because sharing my process and letting you in on my truth is my way of encouraging you to do the same.

The personal experiences I've chosen to share in this book each taught me invaluable lessons and powerful truths. I credit them as the reason I'm the woman I am today. However, not only am I grateful for every step of my journey, it also placed a passion in my heart to do what I can to help others do the same. I'm committed to seeing you healed.

Let's take this journey together.

Are you ready?

Let's go…

P.S. I created a special worksheet to help you take notes and jot down thoughts as we take this journey together. I invite you to go download it at **www.valueinviolation/bonuses**

PART TWO

Treatment

TREATMENT: PHASE ONE

Recovery

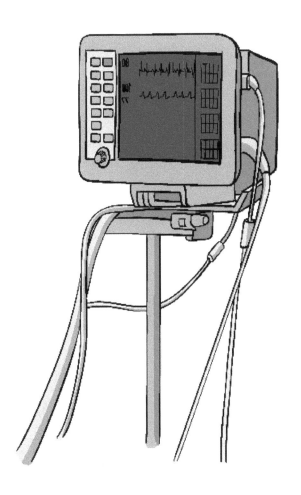

CHAPTER THREE

Reeling

Peek into the Process

I was in my third year of college. Things were going really well. I was excelling in my classes and had just become a member of a prestigious public-service sorority. I also kept busy singing with my college gospel choir and planning events on campus with all the student organizations in which I was involved. Things seemed to actually be going right for me. Two years prior, Lamont had been convicted of molesting another young girl and was sitting in a prison cell somewhere. So even though he hadn't been held accountable for what he had done to me, I had nevertheless been able to get a sense of closure on that whole episode of my life.

I wasn't sure if I had really processed the wound completely, but I was doing everything I could not to let it define me. I was an achiever, a go-getter, and because I felt like my voice hadn't always been heard, I had become a strong advocate for others. I was even majoring in social work.

During that year, however, I struggled to find a church home. It had actually been hard to find one ever since moving away to college. Now, there was definitely no shortage of churches in the area. That was probably part of the problem. I was a small town girl so I didn't want a church that was too intimidating or huge. So when I was invited to a small new church during an event on campus along with a few of my college friends, I jumped on it. After visiting for a couple months, I finally decided to join and make it my new church home.

About a week after I joined the church, my new pastor called me to talk about how I would like to get plugged in and involved in the ministry. He knew I wasn't a, "See you next Sunday," kind of member. I had been really active in all of my previous churches. I sang in the choir, organized programs and often closed the church down. He seemed to appreciate that about me, so he told me he wanted me to keep using my gifts and that I was the "kind of young lady the ministry needed."

A lot of my friends from college had already joined the church over the summer and I was excited to be able grow in my faith alongside them. It was a new church but it was growing really fast. It was nice to be a part of something you felt was going somewhere. All of us were probably drawn to the same things about the ministry. Pastor Thompson was charismatic and could preach you out of your pew, but he was also very approachable and relatable.

When Pastor Thompson called me the next week during the afternoon and asked me to meet him for a ministry-related lunch at a restaurant near my campus, I was open to it, but admittedly wondered if I should question his motives. Ever since I was violated the way I had been at 13 years old, I was a little paranoid about older men and often questioned their motives. I had a wound which left me defensive, cautious and cynical when it came to men, especially older ones. But since he called me on the phone and asked to meet for lunch in an hour, I didn't really have a lot of time to think about it. I agreed and hung up. I just ignored what I thought at the time were paranoid insecurities swirling around in my head. "This man is married, has an infant child and is your pastor. He is not worried about you," I assured myself.

We met for lunch at a casual restaurant near campus and he had his baby daughter with him. She sat so peacefully in her little car seat. I learned then that he was the primary caregiver for her during the day while his wife worked a traditional eight-to-five job. The lunch conversation was a mix of him going on and on about his vision for the church and a "get to know me" session. He asked me questions about my interests, what I was studying and my family. One question that edged on inappropriate but borderline a question an older male friend or relative might ask (he was 39 years old and I was only 20) was, "So why are you single? I'm sure you have all kinds of young men interested in you." I really wasn't expecting that question from him but had used a version of the answer many times before when asked, so my response kind of just rolled off my tongue. "I'm pretty particular with who I attach myself to. I don't plan on just dating a bunch of guys. I'm waiting on the man God has for me."

He sat back in his chair and gave this expression that said I'm impressed. Our lunch meeting ended soon after that.

Fast-forward two weeks.

It was the night of September 24th. The day before was the anniversary date of when I was sexually assaulted at 13 years old. This time of the year had always brought up a lot of memories and feelings, but this year was particularly emotionally difficult. Now I know it was because I was being triggered. See, earlier that evening, Pastor Thompson told me God had shown him I would be his wife one day. Yes, you read that correctly. After I let him know I was uncomfortable with him telling me this and that God wouldn't say something like that, he told me I just didn't have the faith to hear what

God was saying and I was being too serious and too spiritual. That was a low blow. It was a strategic one, too.

Was he being serious? Was he joking? Had he had a fight with his wife and just said that out of frustration? I didn't know. But I was mad that he had put me in the position of having to try to figure it out. Not to mention going on to insult me because I didn't co-sign what he said.

I remember lying in my bed awake late that night. I just couldn't settle my mind. I didn't like how I was feeling. Pastor Thompson had been inappropriate at best but was testing the water to see if I would "bite," at worst. Either way, he had undermined his role as my new pastor. I felt the strong urge to face it head on, get some clarity from him on what he intended, and then from there decide what I would do. So before I closed my eyes that night, I decided the next day I was going to confront him and tell him a few things he clearly had forgotten about being a leader. See, I had evolved into a "fighter" as opposed to a "freezer" over the years. It was my own way of making sure I would never be a victim again. At the time, I thought that was evidence I was dealing with my past. But in reality, it was evidence my past was still dealing with me.

When I woke up the next morning, I was just as unsettled about what Pastor Thompson had told me as I had been the night before. I decided to go through with my plan to schedule a meeting for that afternoon to discuss it with him. When I called, he told me he was working from his home office that day but that a couple of the ministers from the church and the church secretary were there working, too, so I could come by to talk if I needed to. The church was so new that they didn't have their own building yet and shared the sanctuary and administrative offices with another ministry. So some days he worked at the church office and some days he worked from his home office. I knew this was the case, and since there were other church members there, I felt comfortable going by.

I went to my classes that morning and then headed over to Pastor Thompson's house. When I walked in it was uncomfortably quiet. I asked him where everyone was and he said they had, "Just left." I immediately felt like something was off or that he hadn't been honest with me, so I didn't waste any time with small talk and began telling him right away what was on my chest. I let him know I didn't think it was professional and appropriate for him to say I would be his wife one day, whether he meant it literally or any other way. I told him I hoped we could clear the air and be professional from there on out because that was the only way I could continue attending and serving at the church. He responded as if he couldn't believe I had said something he did was out of line and he got very defensive. He didn't apologize for what he said or for how it made me feel. Instead, he said I needed to respect his authority and humble myself.

I was shocked. I couldn't believe my eyes or my ears. I got visibly upset and my voice started shaking as I tried to form my words to respond to him. The problem was, it had become obvious that I couldn't make an argument about how his actions were not in line with the Word of God and expect that line of reasoning to get through to him. In that moment, he was only being driven by his own ego and his flesh. That's when I told him I wanted to leave. "No, you don't need to be driving like this," he said. I leaned against the chair, took a couple of deep breaths and tried to show that I was "fine" so he would just let me leave. But that's when he walked over to me, pulled me close to him and ran his hand down my back.

"This *cannot* be happening…"

I pushed him away and told him to stop and get off of me. He lost his balance a little from my push but quickly regained his footing by grabbing my arm. Then he picked me up, threw me onto the floor, and pinned me to the ground.

"This *is* really happening…"

I started kicking him and trying to push his body off of mine with every ounce of strength I had. I pushed, I hit, I screamed and told him "No!" I told him "Stop!" Nothing I said or did stopped the horror show from happening. Meanwhile, I was having both an internal and an external struggle. So many thoughts were swirling around in my head. I couldn't believe this was happening to me AGAIN. I had committed to being a "good girl" because I was determined not to let what happened to me at 13 make me a statistic. So as a middle finger to Lamont, I had lived my teenage and young adult years on the straight and narrow. I had always worked hard and got good grades in school, was highly involved in my community and church during high school, started preaching at 17, went on a mission trip to Africa at 19 and I was still a virgin at 20…other than when I was raped at 13. I had done all that … only to be raped by my Pastor?! Not to mention it was two calendar days after the anniversary of the date when I was raped the first time. Today was September 25th. I just couldn't believe the irony. It was so *cruel*. I had been betrayed…by Thompson, by God, by myself. As I was thinking about all this, my *body* was being violated but my *soul* was being literally shred apart.

This time, I didn't freeze. I fought like hell. I mean that literally. It felt like I was fighting the devil himself. Thompson's eyes seemed devoid of any humanity and I was no match for what seemed like supernatural strength. I tried as best as I could to defend myself, though. Thompson even mocked me for it. I'll never forget when he said. "At least I'm finally getting some emotion out of you." He seemed to enjoy humiliating and "humbling" me, as he had put it. He was relentless. He only stopped when he got tired of fighting with me.

After I left his house, I wasn't the same young woman I was when I got there. That betrayal broke me into a million pieces. It impacted me in more ways than I could have imagined. My days were no longer individual days, they all just blurred together. I managed to keep my part-time job for three weeks before I just couldn't handle it and quit. I didn't pull my usual A's and B's that semester in college and ended up requesting an "Incomplete" in one class and failing another. Before that incident, I could eat anything I wanted at any time. I was a typical college student and I ate a typical college-student diet. However, for months after that incident, I couldn't eat anything without indigestion and heartburn, and if it had any grease or spice it would make me nauseated. Sleep was also hit or miss.

My entire identity and how I saw my own value had been shaken to the core.

I cried a lot. I broke down a lot. I didn't know how or when my life would get back to any semblance of normalcy. On top of everything, I lost friendships and social support because many of my friends were also connected to the man who wounded me. For months I reeled, wobbled and struggled to stand.

Reeling is a phase that *everyone* whose experienced violation and betrayal has gone through to one degree or another. It's those weeks and months right after you're wounded, right after you're violated or right after someone you trusted hurts you in a way you didn't or couldn't see coming. If you've ever watched boxing, you've seen someone get hit really hard while their guard was down. It's not pretty. They might have stumbled, staggered, spun or even fallen flat on their face.

The immediate response that anyone has after an unexpected hard blow is *reeling*. In the Merriam-Webster dictionary, *reeling* is defined as, "to be in a whirl, to waver or fall back (as from a blow)." Well, the blow in this case is the betrayal, and what comes after it is your mind, body and spirit trying to recover from it. Mental health and trauma professionals call this phase *crisis*.

While you're *reeling*, the effects of the blow you just took can be glaringly obvious.

You may stumble and stagger.

You may struggle to regain your sense of balance.

You may cry a lot...or not at all.

Sometimes your eating and sleeping habits are affected. You might lose your appetite, develop digestive issues or find yourself eating nothing but junk food if you happen to be an emotional eater. Sleep issues and insomnia may show up, as well. Unfortunately, as a result, people's immune systems are weakened, making it much easier to get physically sick on top of being emotionally sick.

This phase is also when we may not have the energy to take care of what seems superficial—like personal hygiene and self-care. We might start letting ourselves or our hair go—or just cutting it off for that matter (think Angela Bassett in the movie *Waiting to Exhale*).

Some people isolate and withdraw from others. Maybe they still show up to work, class or family functions, but they aren't really plugged in to what is going on around them. You can tell they're mentally "checked out."

I've never lost consciousness or went into a coma in real life, fortunately, but it's often described as "blacking out" or "checking out." Doctors sometimes put patients into a coma when an injury is so severe that the brain needs to be shut down in order to improve their chance of survival.[2]

Well, when life hits you hard, similarly to if you were put into a coma, you may check out for a little while in order to use the limited amount of energy you have just to keep your head above water. And that's okay. It's simply how we make sure we survive the painful season we're going through.

This is especially true for those who were in a long-term relationship with an abusive and toxic person. Imagine being betrayed *every day*. When somebody charged with loving and honoring you instead abuses and violates you, it's a betrayal on the deepest level. However, because of the nature of the relationship, sometimes it takes years for a victim to successfully leave the relationship. Those who do are called survivors for a reason. They reeled for months and many times years while in the throes of constant abuse and chronic betrayal.

When you've been betrayed, violated or hurt by another person, but especially by someone you "let" into your life, thoughts and feelings of guilt, anger and shame are *going* to show up. The intensity of these emotions can be so strong that it's hard to contain them. And what happens *then*? Well, some people start projecting their pain toward innocent bystanders and begin lashing out and cutting people with their words so other people can feel as worthless as they feel. Instead of focusing on taking care of their own wound, *some* broken people go around and start bleeding on everyone else.

Most times, however, people don't direct their pain at others. Instead, the aftermath of a relationship wound is often an extremely lonely experience. The battle is often fought completely in the heart and mind of the person who's been betrayed. They keep it all inside. Sometimes out of shame or embarrassment. Sometimes out of fear. Sometimes because the load is so heavy they feel like they can't even lift it enough to hand any of it to anyone else. They carry the pain, shoulder the burden, and experience the flood of emotions all by themselves, and many times with little or no informed guidance or support. The keyword here is *informed*. There won't be a shortage of "advice." Many people will have an opinion on how you are supposed to feel, what you're supposed to do, what you should have done and how they would have done "xyz" if it were them. But if I could have gotten a dollar for every time someone gave me well-intentioned but wrong, misguided or flat out ignorant advice after I was raped, I would be rich today.

You may have had a similar experience. When you're sitting in the middle of your mess, though, it's almost impossible to figure out what advice to keep and what to throw away. Many people are left to try and recover after violation and betrayal without the support, knowledge or tools needed to do so. As a result, some people end up with mental illness, turn to drugs, alcohol or self-injury to cope, lose hope or begin going down a path they were never meant to go.

I'm not sure where you are in your journey right now, whether you are reeling right now or you went through this phase a while ago, but the principles of the **Heal Intentionally Blueprint©** listed below apply just the same. This is what it takes to reel *well*:

Acknowledge the Pain

Being betrayed by someone you trusted hurts…period. It can be a deep aching that can't even be put into words. However, some people feel the need to put on a pretty face and pretend they're fine. Many survivors feel the need to deny they're in pain and prematurely declare, "All is well!" However, we can't heal what we won't acknowledge. Denial serves no one, but it is the *enemy* of broken people who want to be healed.

When we acknowledge our wounds, we begin the process of recovering from them. So don't be afraid or ashamed of them. Acknowledge and express them openly and admit their impact on you.

Accept the Impact

Let's go back to the boxing analogy. After a boxer gets knocked out, the referee starts counting. The boxer has until the count of ten to get back up if he wants to keep fighting. Due to the pressure, many boxers rush to get back on their feet. They may really think they're ready to fight again. So they get back up in order to prove to the referee they could take the blow. But many wobble onto their feet, only to stumble and fall back down shortly thereafter.

When you've been knocked out by deep betrayal, don't rush to try and stand up before you're ready. If you do, you may find yourself wobbling right into another unhealthy relationship or toxic situation. Accept the fact that you've been hit hard and that it might be a while before you're ready to get back into the ring. It's important to give yourself both permission and an opportunity to heal before exposing yourself again.

Anticipate the Win

Hope is what takes us from where we are to where we want to be. When you've been devastated by something or someone in your life, hope may feel out of reach. It's easy to slip into depression and natural to wonder whether you'll get through it. However, it's essential to tell yourself that this incident/situation/circumstance is just ONE round in the fight of your life. There are twelve rounds in a boxing match, and in life we have many more than that. The key is acknowledging you took a hit that knocked you down this round but that the fight isn't over. Trust that in the end you'll win.

Jesus reeled.

He experienced the pain of being betrayed by someone He trusted. Jesus had to come to terms with the fact that Judas, someone He had a close relationship with and trusted, had betrayed Him. He also realized that the time had come that even His Father would have to turn His back on Him. Jesus had no closer relationship with anyone than the one He had with his Father. He enjoyed a perfect relationship with Him. So the notion of His Father turning his back on Him deeply distressed and crushed Him. He expressed the extent of His agony in Mark 14:34 where He says, **"My soul is overwhelmed with sorrow to the point of death."** He grieved so strongly that He literally felt like He was going to die!

Don't ever feel like you're alone in your pain. You're not being dramatic and you're not weak. Being wounded within relationship and betrayed by someone you trusted hurts. Just like Jesus did, acknowledge that pain and admit that it hurts. Honor yourself by not trying to be invincible. If the Son of God was not exempt from being knocked down when hit by such a blow, neither are you.

CHAPTER FOUR

Resting

Peek into the Process

It had been six months since I was raped. My life had been turned completely upside down. I was hobbling through my college courses, trying to keep up with my obligations to the two student organizations I was leading, all while dealing with detectives in the police department. I had decided to try to hold Thompson accountable for what he had done to me. One of the main driving forces behind the decision was that I couldn't bear the idea of another woman experiencing what I had at his hands. So although there was a chance the system would fail me (again) and my pain would be made public, I decided to tell authorities what happened. I cannot explain how I navigated life during this time. It's almost as if I was living on pure adrenaline. I was in survival-mode and trying my hardest to just keep my head above water. For six months I struggled with unpredictable emotions fluctuating from "fine," moving abruptly to apathy, shifting to intense anxiety, jolting to extreme anger, sliding into crippling shame, dipping into deep depression and then circling back to feeling encouraged and affirmed.

I was carrying the weight of my own pain as well as the weight of letting the world (at least my world) know my truth. Sharing my truth meant exposing a man whom many admired and looked up to. Many days I didn't want to face the world or even my own reflection in the mirror. I had no desire to put my betrayal on blast for any and all to see and hear. But deep down I had this sense that God wanted to use me to stand for justice and righteousness, and although I couldn't see it at the time, there was a reason I was going through what I was going through.

The weight was a lot for me to carry at 21 years old and there were many times I just wanted to escape it all. Adrenaline only lasts for so long.

I. Was. Tired.

So after six months of reeling, I decided to rest…intentionally. My best friend and I packed up her car, put our pennies together and drove for ten hours up to St. Louis for a week of rest and relaxation. It was our spring break. I hadn't ever done anything like that—taken a spontaneous road trip out of state. When we left Texas, we didn't even know what hotel we would stay in when we got there. It was kind of huge for me. But I felt a tugging and instinctively knew if I didn't rest, I was gonna lose it.

While driving there, I was reminded of my *autonomy*. That I still owned my body and that I could move without restraint. I was literally moving freely about the country—and trust me, it was like therapy.

During that week I was able to experience silence and hear my own voice. It was quiet enough for me to hear God assure me He was there with me.

By giving myself permission to rest, I was able to slow my mind and quiet my thoughts enough to transition out of crisis and into a place of calm.

The day before we left St. Louis to drive back to Texas, I got a phone call from the district attorneys' office. Thompson had been arrested. The man who had violated me and had *stolen* my sense of freedom had just *lost* his.

It had been six long months, but I felt like I could finally *rest*.

No marathon runner would complete a marathon, cross the finish line and then just decide to keep running for the sake of it. They are able push their bodies and minds to much further limits than most people due to their training, but at some point even they have to stop and rest—or else risk injury, sickness and even death.

However, many people have gone through a *life* marathon, whether it was a divorce, an abusive or toxic relationship, spiritual abuse or sexual assault—only to keep running. They keep living their life, plucking along, trying not to think about it, in hopes it'll just fade into the background. Maybe you've been guilty of this. It's easy to do…even logical. Your kids depend on you. Your job expects you to show up and perform. Your friends' or family members' needs don't stop just because you've been hurt. You've got to keep it moving…right?

If you've thought these thoughts, I don't blame you. However, if you've been reeling from a relationship wound, the natural and necessary next step is to rest. If you're running on emotional fumes, how can you be an available parent? Dependable friend? Attentive partner? Faithful believer?

The answer is you can't. It's impossible.

You only have a limited supply of emotional energy. When you use up all of your available emotional energy and don't or can't move on to the *Resting* phase you end up with the same symptoms you would after a few days of no sleep. I remember when I tested the limits of sleep deprivation, pulling all-nighters back in my college days. After just an hour or two of sleep, I woke up feeling delirious, light-headed, queasy and dizzy.

Sleep deprivation can have serious effects on your health. If you were to go too long without sleep, you may start having issues with your memory, hand-eye-coordination and even your senses of smell and vision.[3] In other words, deprive yourself of sleep long enough and you'll start losing touch with reality.

Why do you think some people who've gone through an extreme trauma "lose it" after a few months? To put it simply, it is their inability to shift from *Reeling* to *Resting*.

However, and this is important, *Resting* after suffering a relationship wound goes way beyond the physical act of sleeping.

Here are 4 ways you are encouraged to Rest as outlined in the **Heal Intentionally Blueprint©**:

Rest Your Mind

When you're hurting, your thoughts are louder than usual. This is because your brain is working overtime to try and make sense out of what happened to you. When you've developed a relationship with someone built on trust, your brain could have hundreds or thousands of memories about that person stored within it. Then the betrayal happened and new memories come into existence that totally contradict the ones already there. Of course, your brain gets confused, but will always try to understand it. This is especially true if you are actually wracking your brain trying to understand WHY. You are literally overworking your brain. This is because you're telling your brain to make sense out of something senseless. Here is a hard truth ... some things just don't have a logical reason for happening. Somethings in life just happen ... because *life*. Give yourself permission to not have all the answers about what happened or what will happen and to just live in today. Allow yourself to be mindful and present in the moment.

This brings me to one of the most important techniques for resting your mind...*silence.* As I mentioned earlier, it was in silence that I was able to hear my own voice again. It is silence that gives you a chance to catch your breath. Studies have shown that silence is an effective way to reduce stress and relieve tension.[4] Quieting your mind is how you rest your mind.

Rest Your Heart

Your heart is the rhythm-keeper. It keeps your blood flowing at the right speed, keeps your organs functioning properly and keeps you alive as a result. Additionally, according to Heart Math Institute, the heart is a complex information-processing center that communicates with your brain and affects mental clarity, emotional balance and personal effectiveness.[5] So when your heart, both literally and figuratively, is out of sync, your life is out of sync.

When you go through something painful like a wound within a relationship, it's heart-breaking. A broken heart has a hard time doing one of its main jobs...managing your emotions. Why do you think your emotions are all over the place when you've been betrayed by someone you trusted? Well, just like what happens to your brain, your heart gets confused by the wound and the signals it's receiving are not in alignment with the baseline input it's used to.[6] In other words, your heart is saying "What you are feeling right now is not normal and I don't know how to process it."

One technique to practice resting your heart is *self-regulation.* Self-regulation is adjusting your thoughts and behaviors based on internal factors even if external factors haven't changed. You do this in order to put yourself in a better emotional state, even if it's only temporary.[7] In simple terms, that means thinking and doing something different in order to feel something different. It gives your heart a chance to temporarily experience positive emotion. The more emotionally healthy and resilient you are, the more you can self-regulate. Trauma hijacks your ability to self-regulate.[8] So a huge part of overcoming trauma is regaining that ability. When you rest your heart (i.e. manage your emotions) it "increases [your] capacity to prepare for, recover from and adapt in the face of stress, adversity, trauma or challenge."[9]

Rest Your Body

Your body is a temple. It houses your mind, spirit, heart and soul. So it comes as no surprise that your body's appearance and functioning takes a hit as well when you've been wounded by someone close to you or that you trusted.

Your body gets its cues from and is in a weird co-dependent relationship with your emotions. This is why you see people with emotional disorders who develop stomach ulcers, have chronic headaches or experience unexplained pain or ailments in their bodies. The reality is that a bad break-up, complicated divorce, toxic relationship or sexual/physical violation will cause emotional disorder. It might not be severe enough to be what mental health professionals refer to as "clinical level" but your emotions will definitely be out of order. And your body will respond accordingly.

This makes taking care of your body one of the most powerful things you can do to shift to the *Resting* phase of your healing process. It will definitely be difficult when you are in the throes of your pain, but trying your best to eat a balanced diet and getting a reasonable amount of sleep will go a long way toward healing. Also, moving your body is therapeutic in the aftermath of trauma.[10] Taking a brisk walk, a dance class, or just dancing alone in your living room gets your blood flowing and produces helpful endorphins that can improve mood.

Listening to your body and finding ways to support it while you do the work of healing your wound(s) sets you up to prevent long-term physical health issues and improves your chances of a successful healing journey overall.

Rest Your Spirit

Your spirit is the most powerful, capable, conscious and connected aspect of you. When you were violated, hurt or betrayed by someone you trusted, by definition, someone took your power and capability to control an outcome that directly impacted you. Not only that, but some wounds are so painful they cause you to disconnect from your conscious because it's just too scary to let yourself feel all the emotions you're experiencing without feeling like you'll "lose it,"—as we discussed earlier. Violation and betrayal wreak havoc on your spirit by their very nature.

The way you rest your spirit is by yielding. Yielding is not resigning. Yielding is trusting. Yield to God and rest in Him. Even though you don't understand the why and may be struggling to trust anything or anyone further than you can throw them, your spirit needs you to trust that although it may be broken right now, it will be put together again.

One of the most powerful ways to rest your spirit is by praying. Prayer is an outlet, a connection and a source of clarity all at the same time. When

> *Prayer is an outlet, a connection and a source of clarity all at the same time*

you are being bum-rushed by emotions due to the hurt you're feeling, you need an outlet. When you are feeling isolated and alone because it seems like no one gets it, you need connection. When you are getting contradictory advice and struggling to know what to do next, you need clarity.

The word spirit comes from the Latin word *spiritus* which means *breath*.[11] Your spirituality is your breath. It keeps you alive. Taking care of it is essential and required to survive.

Rest isn't *optional*. People cannot survive without it in the physical sense and neither can we in an emotional sense. When you choose to rest, you're choosing to acknowledge what you need today in order to have a better tomorrow.

Jesus rested.

When he felt overwhelmed by the pain of betrayal and anxious about what lay ahead for him, he rested...intentionally. In Matthew 26:36a it says, **"Then Jesus went with his disciples to a place called Gethsemane, and He said to them, "Sit here while I go over there and pray."** He realized that the weight of what he was carrying was too heavy for him to bear in His human condition. He needed rest.

He rested his mind when he sought out silence. He rested His heart when He created a moment of peace in order to try and get a hold on his emotions. He rested his body when He fell to the ground in exhaustion. He rested his spirit when He passionately prayed to His Father.

It's okay to say you're tired. It's all right to say you're exhausted. Hurt does that. The pain is real and so is the need to just stop and take care of you. Put *you* first. Make *you* and *your* survival priority.

CHAPTER FIVE

Receiving

Peek into the Process

Have you ever been so exhausted that when you so much as see your bed its *over*? You don't waste any time taking off your shoes or changing out of your clothes. Instead, you just collapse face first, legs sprawled in whichever direction you land. There may or may not be a pillow or comforter involved. Five seconds later and it's a wrap. End. Scene.

Just think back to the last time you needed sleep that bad. That's what St. Louis had been for me. It felt like I'd finally fallen asleep after six months of insomnia. I remember lingering in that "resting" place for a couple weeks, even after I came back from my trip. I slowed down. I let go of the pressure I had been putting on myself to be the "strong black woman." I took a step back from trying to be at every event my student organizations hosted. I stopped trying to be everything to everybody, despite not having anything to give at the time. I accepted the fact that I was broken. I needed and wanted to be put back together again, but I knew I couldn't do it by myself.

Then all of a sudden it was like I woke up from a long nap and realized I was starving … literally starving. I needed nourishment. I needed to be fed. So I started looking around for the people who were supposed to pour into my life. I was ready to *Receive*.

When my friend told me about a women's empowerment conference happening Mother's Day weekend, I thought it was the perfect opportunity for me to hear encouraging teaching and be around women who could speak into my life. I desperately needed it.

I decided to go. It was *amazing*. I learned, laughed and cried. I was encouraged and strengthened by the speakers, the singing and the interactions I had with the other women there. I felt like my tank was being filled up. The female pastor who hosted the conference had such a sweet spirit and the words she shared that weekend have stuck with me to this day. She had a goal of making the women who came to the conference feel like the queens they are, so the last day of the conference included an elegant formal lunch where there was a seat reserved for every woman in attendance. We were graciously served a delicious three-course meal by the hotel wait staff. At the time, I didn't realize why that lunch meant so much to me. But now I know it's because for the first time since having my dignity stolen from me, I felt honored. I felt cherished. I felt *safe*.

The amazing woman who hosted the conference, Pastor Sonjia, became a mentor of mine after that day. I began visiting the church where she and her husband led together. For a while she mentored me from afar as an anonymous member of the congregation. Eventually, I shared my story with her. After that, she took me under her arm, held me close, and didn't let go.

During this step in my journey I also received counseling through my college. My assigned counselor was sweet and soft-spoken. She didn't tell me what to feel and what to think. She listened. She told me how I was feeling was normal. She reminded me it wasn't my fault, something I knew from a logical standpoint but still desperately needed to hear.

Letting my professors know what was going on with me was hard. I was failing one of my classes and struggling in most of them. I wasn't used to struggling in my studies. I had a severe case of "oldest-child syndrome "which means I had been an over-achiever since birth. I both credit and blame my parents for that. I had never gotten less than a "B" throughout my entire time in college until *life happened* and yanked the rug right out from under me.

The last few months had been so rough that sitting down and writing ten to twenty page research papers was next to impossible. My brain had been so foggy that I'd study, but then during my tests the answers were nowhere to be found. My mind would often just go blank. I was a social work major, though, so all of my professors were social workers themselves. In their classes, they had taught me all about trauma, human behavior, mental health and how to help others go through difficult times. They were equipping me to go out into the world as a social worker myself in a few short months, but here I was coming to them in the midst of my own trauma needing their help if I was going to graduate. It was hard for me to ask them for help and especially hard to tell them why I needed it. But to my surprise, they all did everything they could to support me. They gave me extra time, extra credit and even waived some assignments for me. They lifted my arms up, wrapped them around their necks and ran with me across the finish line. I was going to graduate after all.

Their kindness and empathy during that time will never be forgotten. When I applied for graduation at the end of that semester, it felt like I had won that round in the fight of my life. At this point in my journey I was starting to be hopeful that better days were ahead and this season of my life had a purpose. I just had to keep walking it out, trusting myself and trusting God. As I clicked "Submit" on my application, a new personal mantra came into my mind that I still carry with me to this day—"My wounds won't win…I will."

Receiving is like eating breakfast after a long night of sleep. It's the necessary fuel to equip and sustain you for the rest of your healing journey. Allowing yourself to *receive*, which pushes you to *trust* at least a little bit, is the only way you can ever access true healing.

There are a few obstacles that stop a lot of people from going through this phase of the process. Amongst them are *fear* and *shame*. Fear can be paralyzing. It can keep you stuck. Sometimes in our attempt to control things due to our fears, we end up inviting fear to control us instead. Its first cousin *shame* will cause people to suffer in silence rather than reveal that someone they trusted brought them harm. Shame breeds secrecy. Shame breeds dysfunction. Shame breeds self-hate. It tells people lies—like what happened is their fault and that they deserve whatever hurt they're feeling. Again, these are lies and the truth is nowhere in them.

Another obstacle that can prevent people from navigating through this phase of the healing journey is none other than *pride*. Now it may be hard to believe that someone who is broken and struggling with their self-esteem can struggle with pride. However, betrayal takes so much of someone's dignity and pride that the little bit that is left is sometimes held onto so strongly you'd think it was their last dollar. So in attempt to hold onto the *piece* of pride they have left, they try and prove to themselves that *they've got this*. To them, it *ain't nobody's business*. So they build walls around their hearts and move on with life, appearing as strong as ever, while in actuality they are walking around as empty vessels. When people remain weak and empty because they need nourishment but are too proud to ask for some, they sabotage their own healing process.

Yet another obstacle that prevents some people from successfully *receiving* the education, advocacy and support they need after going through a trauma in their lives is a societal-level issue. There simply aren't enough social service agencies, advocates, resources, free counseling services, mentoring programs, access to health-care and churches who reach outside their walls, nor are there enough public policies/laws on the books to reach everyone who needs it.

As a social worker, I've seen firsthand the gaps in care when it comes to domestic violence victims. I've seen the shortage of resources and services for abuse, sexual assault and human trafficking victims. I've personally witnessed so many people who desire counseling after a rough divorce or after leaving a toxic relationship, ministry or workplace who were unable to find affordable and quality counseling. There are many wonderful agencies and organizations doing great work out there, but they need more help and we need more of them. As a society, we must do better in order to create a healthier environment for all of us.

I'm not sure if you're struggling with any of the obstacles I listed above. If so, you're in good company. That makes you human. However, I believe you're reading this because you don't want your wounds to rob you of whatever goals, dreams and desires you have for your life. You're also willing to see what you can do to be intentional about creating an atmosphere in your life where that can happen. Your openness to exploring yourself and seeing where there may be gaps or unresolved issues means you're willing to reach outside of yourself in order to access what you need.

When I realized I was emotionally starving and that I needed certain people in my life in order to heal, grow and rise above what had happened to me, there were certain roles different people played in that process. Of course, I didn't notice all of this at the time, but each of their roles were necessary in order for me to get what I needed to be sustained for the journey.

There are certain things we *all* need in order to be sustained for the journey. According to the blueprint we should:

Receive Medicine

The Merriam-Webster dictionary defines "medicine" as, "The science and art of dealing with the maintenance of health and the prevention, alleviation or cure of disease."[12] When we have an infection or pain in our body that just won't go away, we have no problem calling up our doctor and getting treatment and advice on how to feel better. However, when it comes to matters of the heart and mind, many people never see a doctor, therapist or other medical or mental health professional to address their disease. When we do that, we treat the wounds impacting the heart and mind as if they aren't "real" wounds when, in fact, the pain is just as real—and consequences of not addressing those wounds can be just as dire.

As a social worker, obviously I'm a huge fan of supportive counseling and therapy when experiencing difficult life events. I believe a well-trained counselor or therapist can provide the education and tools you need to cope with crisis, the process to do the work of healing and strategies to help you live your life in your new normal. Professionals such as massage therapists, chiropractors, or holistic health practitioners can help you care for your body while you're doing the work of healing your heart. And although this is not the case the majority of the time, I need to say that I encourage people to be evaluated by a psychiatrist for possible medication management if they're unable to function in their daily life at all or they're experiencing certain severe symptoms—such as suicidal thoughts, psychosis or thoughts of hurting someone, or exhibiting concerning behaviors such as self-injury, extreme recklessness or other deeply concerning behaviors. There are also certain people in this world who are professionally trained and gifted in the area of healing. Make sure you have people like this on your team.

Receive Mentoring

When you've been betrayed by someone you trusted, it inevitably makes it hard to know whom to trust, and you may even struggle with *wanting* to trust. This is absolutely normal, especially at the beginning and right after you're hurt. However, as I discussed earlier, *Receiving* is fuel we need in order to move beyond surviving and toward thriving. A mentor is someone who can help you do that.

Mentors push you forward and don't allow you to stay stuck. They speak life into you when you may be struggling with hopelessness. They help you stay focused on your future and don't let you be taken off course by "brokenness fog" (oh it's a real thing … believe me!). The relationship you have with them also gives you an opportunity to have someone in your life that actually has your best interests in mind and genuinely desires to see you happy and well. This is very valuable, especially if you've recently left or been hurt by someone who didn't have your best interests in mind and instead did everything they could to hurt you. However, one of the greatest assets a good mentor has is wisdom. Sound wisdom in a season of brokenness is priceless. It feeds you, supports you and guides you.

Sound wisdom in a season of brokenness is priceless.

As you saw in my story, finding my mentors in that season was exactly what I needed to keep me moving forward. The wound I experienced could have sent my life in a totally different direction, but connecting to mentors who saw my purpose beyond my pain prevented that from happening. That is the reason I started coaching and being a mentor to women who've gone through similar experiences. It is also why I created the ***Heal Intentionally Blueprint©***. If you don't have a mentor today, regardless of your age or stage in life, I suggest you find one. A good mentor doesn't mind getting their hands dirty while helping you dig out of whatever hole that you're in. Then, once you're out, they'll show you how to build something beautiful on top of it.

Although I had some wonderful human mentors, my number one mentor in this season was God. I went to Him with my questions. I looked to Him for my answers. I depended on Him as a shoulder to cry on. If you're a person of faith, know that God is the best mentor you could ever have. He's been where you are, knows who you are and knows where you're going.

Receive Maintenance

Sometimes a loss or wound can be so devastating that you have trouble functioning and doing normal everyday things for a while. During this time, there is absolutely nothing "normal" about your life. If your marriage just ended, your *normal* just ended. If you just left a toxic relationship which had consumed all of your energy, time and resources and you literally don't know what life looks like without that person in it, it may take a while for you to find a *new* normal. If you've experienced something traumatizing like rape or sexual assault, you may wonder if normal will *ever* exist again. When events like these happen in your life, you may need some help taking care of basic needs, tasks and responsibilities for a little while. When you're struggling to simply get up every morning, go to work or school and make it through the day, having people in your life to hold you up and help sustain you is critical.

For me, this looked like the couple of friends who made sure I was okay and regularly called just to check on me. It looked like my professors, helping me with my classwork so that I could still accomplish my goals even though I wasn't at my best. It also looked like my family members, who helped support me financially after I had to quit my job right after the rape, when I just couldn't hold it down anymore.

Maintenance is done to help preserve something of *value*. Usually you think of maintenance done on something like a car or home. However, in this case, we are talking about *you*. You are *valuable*. When you endure a sudden or severe wound, allow people to help you maintain your life until you can get your feet back under you. It helps you share the load so you don't feel like it's yours to carry alone—or possibly drop it all together. These maintenance people can be friends, family, teachers, coworkers or places like domestic violence shelters, social service agencies and churches. They can come in many forms. The key is making sure that you give them the chance to do their work.

Jesus received.

As He experienced the all-consuming pain of betrayal He asked for support outside of himself. Even Jesus called on his friends to help him shoulder the burden of what He was about to face on the cross. This happens in Matthew 26:38b where He speaks to three of his closest friends and disciples and says, **"Stay here and keep watch with me."** Jesus, of course, didn't *need* any help praying to His own Father, but he still asked for it.

In doing this, Jesus modeled for us the importance of being open to Receiving and being willing to ask for help when we're carrying a burden that's heavier than usual. It's not a sign of weakness to acknowledge you can use some help—it's a sign of *wisdom* and acknowledges your humanity.

TREATMENT: PHASE TWO

Re-Assessment

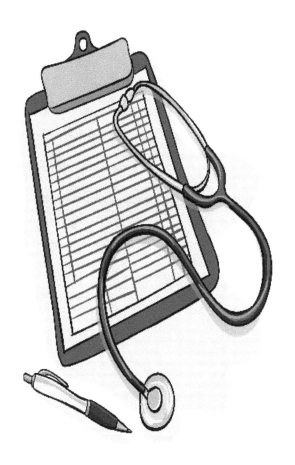

CHAPTER SIX

Reviewing

Peek Into the Process

My normally quiet and empty one-bedroom apartment was packed full of people laughing, hugging and catching up on one another's lives. My family had come in from all over to see me graduate with my Bachelor's degree. There were people crammed on the couch, standing in my kitchen and sitting on the floor along the wall all around the living room. It was nice having all my family there. I couldn't contain myself. I was so happy. I'd done it. I was finally going to get that coveted piece of paper I had worked so hard for the last four years. It was the first time my grandparents and extended family had ever even seen my apartment. As I looked over the room, I couldn't help but start reflecting on how this apartment had been my sanctuary all those many nights I had cried and prayed myself to sleep. When I noticed my couch pillows had been placed on the floor to make more room for people to sit, I remembered the night just days after the assault that I walked through my door filled with so much anger about what was done to me that I'd picked up my pillows, threw them at the wall and accidentally knocked down a picture frame. The clash between this beautiful and joy-filled room and the indescribable pain that had filled it only months prior was so palpable I could feel it.

It made me even more grateful to be walking across the stage that weekend. It was one month shy of a year since my life had been uprooted by deep betrayal. This month, August, was going to be my new beginning. I committed to being intentional about *Reviewing* and reflecting on what I had experienced, how it had impacted me and what I was going to take with me into my future. I wasn't going to let this moment pass.

Reviewing is the part of the journey where you start feeling better. You've gained strength within yourself and from the support you've received from others. You feel stable again and like you're back on your feet. You're not feeling the emotional pain of the wound on a daily basis or at least it is *much* more manageable. Honestly, this is where many people think their healing work is complete. They feel as if they can move on … they're good now. However, this is actually where the real work begins. *Reviewing* is the process of going back over and processing what you have learned and experienced from the betrayal, violation or wound. It's doing the *work*. Don't "complete" your journey before completing the work. If you're

> *Don't "complete" your journey before completing the work.*

reading this book and you're not sure if you've done the work regarding some of your wounds, now is the perfect opportunity to do so.

Do you remember when you were in grade school and the teacher would spend weeks teaching from a few chapters in the textbook? Well after he/she taught you from those chapters, sometimes she would give you a *review*. The review was meant to give you a chance to dive in deeply and focus on what you would be tested on in the future. The review was given so you would know what information you needed to commit to memory and what you could afford to forget. A review was also given because the teacher knew you would be tested and wanted you to pass. It wasn't enough to just show up to class. In order to be sure you could apply the knowledge and go to the next grade *level*, you had to be tested.

Well, when we experience a wound in life, it's no different. There comes a time when we have to go back over what we've learned and determine what we should commit to memory for the future and what we can afford to forget. Although it may seem overwhelming, we have to process it. The struggle is that sometimes even the notion of looking back to when you hurt is so scary or uncomfortable that we just refuse to do it. We'd rather stay in this nice new place of newfound peace. After all, it's the best you've probably felt in months or years. Why disrupt that and return to where you hurt?

On a surface-level, that makes sense, but doing so means your healing will also be surface-level. It won't go deep enough to withstand the test of time. Whenever the next trauma, drama or test happens in your life (which it will), both the fresh new wound and the old wound which had merely healed on the surface-level will hit you like a ton of bricks. That's how it works. When you don't heal completely, your wounds may fade, but they come back around with a vengeance if triggered by a new person or situation revolving around with the same issue.

This happened when I was triggered by Thompson's attempt to manipulate and control me through his words and his abuse of authority as my pastor at the time. I had a wound that thirteen-year-old Chaena never really processed and only healed on a surface-level. Of course, I was a child at the time and to that end, it wasn't my fault nor my choice. However, it was an unresolved wound, nonetheless. The meaning and beliefs I took away from that incident were affecting twenty-one year old Chaena. At thirteen, I processed my wound to mean, "Never *freeze* again." Instead, I had to *fight* and assert myself whenever I felt like I needed to defend my honor. That's why, at 21, I felt like I just HAD to go and confront Thompson after I felt dishonored and disrespected by what he had told me. I could have just ignored the foolery and never returned to my brand new church. And believe me, I dealt with the guilt and shame of even going over there to confront him. I asked "What if?" more times than I can remember. However, the truth is my unresolved wounds had impacted me at a cellular-level. I had lived my life since that first wound with an unwavering need to "prove my value," since it had been stolen, "defend my honor," since I wondered if I had any left and "fight," because "freezing" made me look weak.

I'm sharing my truth with you because I didn't realize the *meaning* and *beliefs* I attached to my first major wound until I went through the *Reviewing* process after my second major wound. I don't want you to make the same mistake of not healing one wound and having it put you at higher risk for being wounded again. Perhaps some of you reading this may even be on your fourth or fifth major wound at this moment. My desire for you is to do the work and heal intentionally so you can stop that cycle. Even if it's scary and even if it's uncomfortable. If you have an unresolved wound, whether it's from last month, last year or last decade … do the work. As I discussed very early on in the book, but that probably makes much more sense now, doing the work is what *stops the bleeding*. It stops the cycle.

Reviewing is the step in the **Heal Intentionally Blueprint©** that is meant to teach you how to *extract wisdom from your wounds*. It gives you a strategy to *assess* your wounds and then *decide* what meaning you want to attach to them. *Reviewing* does rely on evidence-based theories and practices which have shown to be effective in the assessment and treatment of clients by mental health professionals, but it also has been proven to be effective in my own life, as well as in the lives of coaching clients I've worked with.[13] [14] [15] [16] Although it is a powerful strategy, it is not a substitute for therapy. You would actually benefit from working through the strategy with your therapist or counselor if you happen to be working with one. But I want to share this process with you, because just being aware of a strategy that can teach you to extract wisdom from your wounds puts you at the front of the class. So many people don't heal after hurt simply because they don't know how to, not because they don't want to.

If you would like the bonus worksheet to complete the Reviewing exercises, go to www.valueinviolation.com/ bonuses

So let's go ahead and get started …

Step One: Assess the Damage

The first part of assessing a wound is to *look* for it, *acknowledge* it and *be aware* it exists. Sometimes the wound is obvious and you're already aware of it. But some wounds are buried beneath years of denial, suppressed memories, anger and unforgiveness. Sometimes admitting we have an unresolved wound would mean acknowledging that a person still has some level of control over us. Nobody wants to admit to that. However, doing a full assessment, from head-to-toe, like a doctor would do to a gunshot victim, is what's needed in order to make sure nothing goes unnoticed or unaddressed.

Another part of assessing a wound is diagnosing it. You've got to give it a name. Naming something helps you know how to handle it. What kind of wounds do you have? A wound of rejection? A wound of shame? A wound of loneliness? A wound of abandonment? A wound of dishonor? A wound of disloyalty? There are many types of wounds. Each has their own characteristics, symptoms, and appearance. Assessing and diagnosing them is the first step to figuring out what you need to do to heal them.

Step Two: Browse Your Beliefs

Beliefs are those assumptions, thoughts, and ideas which shape and guide how we live our lives. We get our beliefs from our **experiences** and the **meaning** we attach to them. Your brain is like a computer, but even more complex. It stores and files people, events, information and experiences into categories and beliefs for easier recall and so that we don't have to go through life experiencing everything as if it were the first time, every time. It's obviously a *good* thing that we can learn, remember and come up with conclusions about the things we have experienced. However, when you were deeply hurt and experienced the wound that disrupted your entire life, your brain still did its job and came to conclusions about what you should think about yourself, the other person, the situation and even what you should think about the world you live in as a result of it. Sometimes the beliefs we develop after going through hurtful experiences are healthy and helpful, but sometimes the beliefs we develop are unhealthy and unhelpful. They're based on fear, distrust, hurt and confusion. Wherever our beliefs lead, good or bad, our behaviors will follow. However we *believe* is how we *behave.*

   In this step in the process, think hard and dig up the beliefs you came up with in the aftermath of your wound. What beliefs did you develop about yourself, the person or people who betrayed you, people in general, the world you live in and even God, after experiencing the wound(s) you listed in Step 1? What beliefs did you develop about *why* it happened? What did you *tell* yourself after you were hurt? How did you "make sense" of it? Treat your brain like a computer and do some browsing. Search and go into "folders" you haven't opened in a while or forgot were even there.

Step Three: Stop the Self-Sabotage

The reason processing your wound(s) is so important is it gives you a chance to get back in the driver seat of your own thought life. In order to do that, we have to "take captive every thought."[17] Taking captive every thought means "detaining" every thought. When an officer detains someone, they're not under arrest, but they're being held against their will temporarily to give the officer a chance to see if they are up to no good or completely innocent. Once they determine that, the person is either arrested or let go.

Well, in this step of the *Reviewing* process, take a look at all of the thoughts/beliefs you listed in Step 2 and see if the beliefs are true, future-focused, hopeful, healthy and line up with your values. Sometimes we've been telling ourselves certain things for so long that we think they're truth. But just because something has been repeated over and over doesn't make it true. Also, some of the beliefs we carry may have looked like "strengths" but really they were based off of fear of being hurt again. Some of our beliefs exist because of tradition or how we were raised and they've done nothing but keep us stuck in the past.

You deserve to have beliefs that make you feel full of hope and deserving of everything you desire. You deserve a thought life that lines up with what's important to you. You deserve a belief system that works for you and not against you. I encourage you to commit yourself in this moment to the honor and responsibility of detaining every thought. When you can change your thoughts about your life, let alone your thoughts about your wounds, you can and will change your life!

Reviewing is where the work gets done. Being willing to look eye-to-eye with your wounds, naming them and choosing how you're going to think about them is taking your power back. It's how you heal on purpose. It's how you move closer to your purpose, as well. Many times these difficult wilderness seasons lead to a door that will allow access to your purpose. Seeking and gaining understanding of the beliefs you need keep, shift or throw away from a season of wilderness is crucial if you want to live a life of purpose and avoid getting stuck and simply circling around in the wilderness. If you do *Reviewing* well and then go on to make it a regular practice in your life, your life will truly never be the same.

Jesus reviewed.

As Jesus lay in the Garden of Gethsemane praying to God, He acknowledged He was hurting. It seemed as if the weight of the betrayal by Judas and even the reality of what He was about to experience finally hit Him. At that moment, a thought based on fear must have entered his mind, because He prayed, **"Father, if You are willing, take this cup from Me;"** [18] In a moment of humanity, He was fearful, anxious, and thought a thought that clearly didn't line up with what was most important to Him … doing the will of His Father.

However, as you can see, that sentence in scripture ends with a *semicolon*, not a period. A *semicolon* is used to connect two *related* yet *independent* clauses. So that particular semicolon is more than just a random punctuation mark. It shows us that Jesus had a fear-based thought but almost immediately and without much delay He had a totally separate thought and said, **"Yet, not My will, but Yours be done,"** [19] He took that first thought **captive** and **chose** to think about His future and His purpose instead of his current circumstances … as bad as they were.

You can control your thoughts—they don't have to control you. As you walk this journey of healing intentionally, when thoughts come across your mind that don't serve you, take them captive, arrest them, and refuse to let them linger around too long.

CHAPTER SEVEN

Releasing

Peek into the Process

I had both dreaded and looked forward to this day for two years. The day had come for me to face Thompson in a court of law. Once again a major life moment fell during my "favorite" month, September. This time it was the 29th.

The courtroom was sterile, plainly furnished and there was wood paneling everywhere. There was wood in the walls, the pews, the judges bench, the witness stand ... just about everywhere. I'll never forget all that wood. It was pretty quiet, but since the judge hadn't come in yet, and it was a busy morning with multiple cases on the docket. There was a lot of whispering and movement up and down the center aisle. All kinds of people were coming and going, including lawyers, defendants, family members and police officers. Whenever the bailiff walked in the room, it got noticeably more quiet as people recognized he carried with him the authority and accountability which resided in that building.

I sat near the front of the courtroom with two of my best friends on either side of me for moral support. Since Thompson and his lawyer had decided he would plead guilty and accept a plea bargain, the case wouldn't have to go to trial. So today was the plea hearing. I was going to be given the chance to speak directly to Thompson before the court and give a "victim impact statement." It was my chance to tell him, the judge, and everyone who was in the courtroom that day how Thompson's actions had affected me. There were not enough words in the dictionary to fully express how that wound had impacted my life. However, I had finally managed to put a few words together earlier that morning which I'd hand-written on a piece of notebook paper. I held it tightly in my hand and waited for the moment Thompson would enter the courtroom.

All of sudden, there he was.

He walked in and looked straight ahead as he made his way to his seat. His lawyer followed close behind.

This was it.

I had wondered how I would feel when I saw him again. Would anger consume me? Would fear cause me to shrink inside myself? I had no idea. But at that moment, I got my answer. I looked directly at him. I immediately felt my body react to seeing him, but he didn't intimidate me. I had become stronger, not weaker, since he had wounded me. I didn't feel anger toward him, either. All I felt was quiet resolve and sheer gratefulness for being where I was that day compared to where I had been two years prior.

It was weird.

It took being in that courtroom and seeing how I responded to show me that I had released the resentment that I had felt toward him. Not because he *deserved* my forgiveness, but because I wanted to be free. I wanted my power back and I wanted to be healed … for real.

The judge entered the courtroom. "Please rise," the bailiff stated. Everyone in the courtroom stood to their feet. "You may be seated," the judge said. Then the judge presided over two or three other cases on the docket that morning. The next thing I knew, it was time for our case. The judge called out the case name and number. Thompson and his lawyer stood up. The judge then asked Thompson if he was prepared to plead guilty to the charges while being fully aware of his rights, and that he was doing so of his own free will. Thompson responded with three simple yet significant words. "Yes, your Honor."

After that, the judge allowed me to come forward and give my victim impact statement. Random people from all walks of life who filled that courtroom suddenly became a part of my healing process. They didn't know me from Eve, but I told them exactly what had happened to me. I shared with them how it had impacted me. Most importantly, I let them know that although I still struggled some days, I knew my wounds had a purpose and they were well on their way to being healed. While giving that statement to a room full of strangers, I was able to release guilt and shame. I looked straight into the eyes of the man who had caused me so much pain and let go of anger and resentment. And when I walked out of that courtroom, I went ahead and left the fear and self-doubt behind. What did I need to fear and why should I continue to doubt myself? With God's help, I was facing a wound that was meant to *break* me and instead I was letting it *build* me. I could only go up from here.

Let it go. Easier said than done, right? Well it depends on what you decide "it" is. When you've experienced loss, hurt or betrayal, *let it go* sounds a lot like *forget about it* or *get over it*. It can sound like giving the person who wounded you a pass or putting your own pain on the back burner as if it's not valid or real. Well that's not what *it* really is. Letting it go or *Releasing* is simply the act of consciously *choosing yourself*. It's the decision to lie down and leave behind anything that isn't going to get you healed, free, and whole. *Releasing* is the step in your journey that shifts you from surviving to thriving. It's also the step where you start to become the woman you need to be in order to manifest the healthy and fulfilling life and relationships you deserve.

Of course, much of what you have to release after experiencing betrayal isn't something you can do overnight. Many times it's a process, or even a daily decision. But the decision you'll be making is the decision to put you and your purpose at a higher priority than your pain or the person who wounded you. That's *what* you're deciding. Now, *why* you're deciding is different for every person. Your *why* might be your children, your peace, your faith or your desire for a healthy and loving relationship in the future. It may be all of those or perhaps a completely different reason. But the point is…remind yourself of your *why* so that you can maintain the courage and endurance to *release* even when it's difficult.

It's crucial that you understand that *Releasing* doesn't demand that you *forget* about what happened to you. Instead it invites you to create space in your heart for healing to take place. In this step of your journey, you choose to release those unwanted thoughts, emotions and behaviors you may have realized were present during the *Reviewing* phase. You choose to release anything and anyone that would keep you bound, stuck and broken, so that you can open yourself up to receive the wholeness, health and freedom you desire.

So now to the important part…here's exactly what you have to *release* in order to *Heal Intentionally*:

Release the G.A.S.

Okay, I know what you're thinking. Don't worry… I'm not talking about *that* kind of gas. Although when we carry (G)uilt, (A)nger and (S)hame around with us, we may as well be walking around full of it—gas that is. Guilt, anger and shame make you uncomfortable, unpleasant to be around and leave little room for much of anything else. Nobody likes being gassy, and nobody wants to be around a gassy person. You have to view guilt, anger and shame the same way. Do everything you can to work through it and eventually work it out of your system. The moment you do, you'll feel lighter and able to move forward in your healing journey without carrying around the extra weight.

I released the G.A.S. in my own life, not just because I wanted to, but because I had to. I couldn't take it anymore. I couldn't keep living in the shadows…hiding because of shame. It was suffocating. I wanted to breathe freely so I could move freely. Don't be ashamed of the scars your wounds have left. Instead, wear them as a badge of honor. You survived.

I invite you to release the G.A.S. from your own life even as you read these words. Relinquish them of their power once and for all.

Release the Habits

Habits are those things we do to pass the time, keep ourselves busy or help us to forget what is really going on in our lives… even if just for a moment. Habits like drinking alcohol, using drugs or over-eating are common ones that hurting people use to self-medicate their emotional pain. But sneaky and subtle ones like sabotaging relationships so you always get them before they can get you, being indecisive or even being an extreme "people-pleaser" so people don't have a reason to dislike you are ALL habits we need to release in order to be free. These habits are things we do to try and control our lives but end up actually controlling us.

In my teenage and young adult years, I had made a habit of seeking achievement and people-pleasing at the expense of seeking healing and focusing on what *I* needed. However, when I began to release the need to be validated by others and stopping being ashamed of my story, that's when I felt my life shift.

You can have people in your life that are like habits too. Healing *on* purpose and *for* purpose involves taking a hard look at the people in your life and determining whether or not they are supposed to be in your life. When you've been hurt in the area of relationships, you may struggle with not wanting to tackle this issue. But releasing all toxic, codependent, or unfruitful relationships is a critical part of guarding your heart and moving toward manifesting the relationships you deserve.

I want to encourage you to let go of any habits you may be holding onto that are serving as nothing but emotional crutches. You use them to hold yourself up because you feel like you'll fail or fall apart without them. You may have depended on them for a long time, but if you've done the work up to this point, you're ready to walk on your own two feet.

Release the Clutter

Clutter makes any space unappealing, uninviting and unproductive. It makes it hard to see, hard to focus and hard to move. Clutter creates chaos and lack of direction. But the scariest part is that if you stay in a cluttered environment long enough, you can start getting so used to it that clutter becomes your comfort zone. If you've ever watched the TV show *Hoarders*, you know this to be true. You don't ever want to get to that point.

In order to heal intentionally, the clutter you need to release is composed of negative thinking, fear, rejection and self-doubt. These four issues clutter up your mental and emotional space. They make it hard to operate from a place of truth and impossible to develop a sense of clarity.

Fear and self-doubt keeps you stuck mentally, emotionally, in your relationships and ultimately in every area of your life. They make you question and doubt almost every decision you make. Sometimes fear cripples you to the point where life becomes something that just *happens* to you as opposed to being something you play an active role in *creating*. It's easy to see how taking a backseat in your own life makes it hard to have a say on where you'll end up. *Releasing* fear and self-doubt is the first step to regaining control of your life.

Negative or "stinking thinking" affects how you see everything around you. This is because everything is filtered through a lens of expected failure. Whatever you think is what you become. When you're overwhelmed by stinking and small thinking, it's impossible to win in any area of your life.

Rejection attacks your self-esteem and your identity. When you don't know who you are, other people will define you. When you don't know how much you're worth, other people will decide that for you. As you can see, dealing with rejection can cause you to attract people who will use you, abuse you and then eventually reject you. I will say that feeling rejected is a natural response to experiencing abandonment and betrayal. This is because betrayal is rejection in the simplest terms. However, being rejected doesn't mean you *become* rejected. I hope you see the difference there. What someone does to you doesn't mean it needs to *become* you. When you allow what happens to you to become you, you risk continuing the cycle.

Release the Resentment

This is officially one of the hardest yet most freeing steps in the healing journey. Releasing the resentment deals with the powerful concept of forgiveness. When someone betrays your trust and turns your world upside down *on purpose*, the anger and rage is real. It is so real you can feel it in the very depths of your being. I know. However, the damage that lingering unforgiveness can do to our heart, body and soul is just as real. Unforgiveness hardens your heart, causes dysfunction in your body and chips away at your soul.

Unforgiveness demands that you stay where you are and refuse to leave the place you were hurt. In order to stay in a state of unforgiveness you have to stay mentally and emotionally connected to the original pain. Unforgiveness isn't always a conscious decision we make. Sometimes we don't even realize we have unforgiveness in our hearts. However, whether you realize it or not, the impact it has on you is the same.

This is where healing intentionally comes into play. You can make the conscious decision to explore your heart and see if any unforgiveness is still living there. And although forgiveness doesn't happen just because we want it to, making the decision daily and setting an intention to forgive jump-starts the process. This reminds me of one my favorite quotes I learned from one of my mentors, Pastor Sonjia. "Whatever you do in repetition becomes your persuasion." When you decide to walk in forgiveness every day, eventually unforgiveness will have to release its grip for good.

Naturally, you may be wondering who you'll need to forgive. If so, it's understandable. The truth is that when betrayal happens, there is plenty of hurt and blame to go around.

The first person we have to forgive is the **Betrayed**. That's you—the one who was hurt. Many times this is harder than expected because we can be so tough on ourselves. But in order to be free, you have to release any blame you've put on yourself for your role in the wound. Guilt has to go and unrelenting self-love has to take its place.

The next person to forgive is the **Betrayer**. That's the person or people who hurt you. They may not even have asked for your forgiveness. They didn't earn nor do they "deserve" your forgiveness. However, *you* deserve to forgive them because you've done the work. And you're worth it. Letting them go doesn't mean you're letting them off the hook or minimizing the damage they did. But by releasing resentment toward them, you are choosing to live again and denying them any more permission to influence your life.

The last people to forgive are the **Bystanders**. These are the people who were indirectly involved in the hurt and betrayal. These people come in many shapes or forms. They could be the person your spouse cheated on you with or the family member who made excuses for and took the side of your abuser. They could be the people who didn't believe you when you told them what happened or who said hurtful things to you out of ignorance. It can be easy to forget about the need to deal with the feelings we feel toward *bystanders* because they weren't directly involved. But intentionally forgiving them is part of the process and leaves no stone unturned. You can't give unforgiveness any ground to take root and continue to grow in your life.

This step of the healing process is primarily about releasing the lie that when you were violated, you somehow lost some of your value. The opposite is true—and it's the inspiration behind the title of this book. Not only are you valuable in spite the violation, but there is value **in** the violation. In fact, God uses "crushing" moments in our lives as an opportunity to show us the value we possess. In order to extract its valuable oil, an olive is put under immense pressure and *crushed* in below freezing temperatures. Any person with purpose and who is called to significance will have to experience brokenness. It's a prerequisite to greatness.

Jesus released.

The journey to the cross involved a lot of crushing. Jesus was betrayed, beaten, mocked, ridiculed and finally hung on a cross. If He would have wished that each of his accusers, abusers and bystanders who beat and mocked him be given a one-way ticket to hell, I think most of us would have understood.

But, instead of having anger and resentment toward them, in Luke 23:34, Jesus says, **"Father, forgive them, for they do not know what they are doing."** He operated in *radical forgiveness*. He forgave those who hurt him and felt no resentment toward those who stood by and watched as it all took place. Now, it wasn't because any of them deserved to be forgiven. He released them because he didn't want *unforgiveness*, which is a sin in God's eyes, to prevent Him fulfilling his purpose.

There's that *purpose* word again. You may be wondering why I keep mentioning purpose. It's important because your purpose is the sole reason you exist in this world. Unforgiveness holds your purpose hostage. When you take your purpose and put it next to unforgiveness, purpose has to win every time. You, my friend, have a divine purpose. The hurt you experienced may have been soul-crushing and turned your life completely upside down, but know that it didn't destroy your purpose. Your purpose is still strongly intact. All you have to do is *Release* so you can keep moving closer to fulfilling it.

TREATMENT: PHASE THREE

Rehabilitation

CHAPTER EIGHT

Restoring

Peek into the Process

After that season of releasing and letting go, I felt lighter. It was as if a giant weight had been lifted off of my chest. I felt as if I could just go, and the truth is, I actually wanted to run. I felt healthier and stronger. I had this sense of urgency to move into whatever was next. I wanted and needed to meet the future me. I wanted to see what kind of woman would emerge after all of the drama and trauma. However, I wasn't willing to just wait around and be an observer in my own life. I became intentional about my personal growth and began an *unrelenting pursuit of purpose.*

I read dozens of personal development books in the second half of 2009. I spent more time praying and reading scripture than I ever had in my entire life. I filled journal after journal with notes from the books I was reading and highlights from the teachings and sermons I was hearing. In my journal, I'd also write out my prayers and reflections because it made them tangible. It made them real. I went to conferences and

THE VALUE IN VIOLATION

attended events so I could place myself in environments that would grow and stretch me.

A really vivid memory I have from this part of my healing journey happened right around New Years in 2010. My church was celebrating the New Year with a church-wide fast and prayer event. Everyone who took part in it was encouraged to commit to fasting for 21 days from 6am to 6pm as a way of intentionally seeking God and gaining clarity about their lives. I was already being radical in my pursuit of purpose at the time so I took on the challenge. Why not?

Well, one night during the fast, I was home alone in my apartment, lying on the couch and using YouTube as my entertainment for the evening. As I skipped around from video to video, I realized that one particular area of my life was a sore spot. It always had been. That was the area of *relationships*. A few weeks earlier I had dipped my toe back into dating. After a few dates I realized the guy looked good on paper but had no substance and wasn't looking for what I had to offer. He also didn't like that my body wasn't something I was willing to offer until marriage. This had been the story of my life. I was content being single, but I did desire to be married. I knew he would have to be a special guy, given my past experiences, and I couldn't wait to meet him.

As my mind drifted out of "la la land" and back to my computer, I saw a video link over to the side of my screen that caught my eye. It dealt with the issue of seeking the approval of people through your achievements, accolades or membership in certain groups or organizations. It tackled the topic of *people-pleasing*… something I had struggled with since I was thirteen years old. My sense of self-worth had been deeply affected by wounds and I had come to believe I could only prove I had value and significance by racking up achievements. But that night, while watching the video series, I realized the truth is that my value had never been diminished or lessened. I was always highly valuable to God and my accomplishments were just a by-product of the gifts He had placed on the inside of me.

That night was a major turning point in my life. Wrapped in a blanket, alone in my apartment and browsing YouTube, God had found a way to share His heart with me. By this point in my journey He had restored my joy, my trust, my hope and my identity. I knew now more than ever who I was and Whose I was. I knew He had plans for me...plans to give me hope and a future.[20] I had come to realize the area of my deepest pain was really just a door to my divine purpose.

Restoring is the step in the healing journey where you'll start hoping and dreaming again. You will have done enough of the healing work that you'll begin to reap the benefits. Many people regain interest in things they hadn't even let cross their mind in a while, such as a new career/business, relationship or hobby. There's often a renewed sense of urgency to pursue your passions and your purpose. This step in your journey shows you there is "Life after _____." Just fill in the blank with whatever or whoever was the source of your wound. You realize that better days are ahead of you. And ultimately, you get your smile back. Anyone who has been through brokenness and betrayal gets how amazing it feels to be in a space and place to be able to smile from their soul again.

As a believer, *Restoring*, for me, involved the spiritual practices of prayer and fasting in addition to reading personal development books, attending conferences and even applying for graduate school. However, this part of the journey looks different for every person. The principle and universal truth of the *Restoring* step is that it is the result of *unrelenting pursuit*. In order to heal intentionally, you must participate in your own process. You have to read the books and educate yourself about what you've gone through and how to overcome, you have to show up to the coaching and therapy sessions, and you have to do those things like journal, meditate and practice self-care. True healing is not something that just happens *to* you, it also happens *through* you. And just a word of wisdom for believers who are "waiting" on God to reach down and heal you—even in the Bible healing was always a contact sport requiring the people who wanted to be healed to put some "skin in the game." The lame man had to *pick up* his mat, the leper had to *dip* in the Jordan River seven times and the woman with the issue of blood had to *touch* the hem of Jesus' clothes. These are just a few examples found in scripture. But as you can see, however you slice it, healing requires intention and purposeful action.

> *True healing is not something that just happens to you, it also happens through you.*

When you've walked through each of the first five steps of the **Heal Intentionally Blueprint©**, restoration will happen naturally. In this step of the journey you can expect to:

Restore Your Joy

You'll be in a better place emotionally. The anxiety, sadness or depression you may have felt earlier in your journey will lift and you'll begin to feel lighter on your feet. As I mentioned earlier, you'll get your smile back. Joy, which is something that radiates from the inside out, will become a new source of strength that will energize you to keep you pressing forward and build the life you deserve.

Restore Your Trust

After being wounded I'm sure trust had *left* the building. You probably didn't know if it would ever return. But there's something about seeing yourself grow and accomplish your goals that causes you to trust in your own abilities again. Then, the more you trust yourself, the more goals you accomplish. In the mental health field, a term often used to describe this concept is "self-efficacy"[21] However, as you heal, not only will you trust *yourself* again, but then you'll also begin to trust *others* again. Your heart will be whole enough to handle vulnerability, but also wise enough to know who does and who doesn't deserve it.

Restore Your Hope

Hope allows you to have vision and to dream about what lies ahead. Without vision, you're not living, you're simply existing. Without the ability to dream, you can't create what you desire, you can only accept things as they are. The truth is, you were created to be a *creator* and a visionary, but trauma serves as a thief that *steals* our vision and then attempts to *subvert* our purpose. So restoring your hope is a critical part of the healing journey. In this step of the process, you regain a sense of *say so* about what happens in your life. You take back what trauma and devastation had stolen.

Restore Your Health

When you experience disruption in your life by way of abuse, brokenness or betrayal, every aspect of your being is impacted. This includes your physical body. Your body can become unpredictable and unrecognizable when it's put under enough stress and pressure. Digestive issues, chemical and hormonal imbalances and even unexplained pain can become a part of everyday life. But the good news is, when you get to *Restoring*, you begin to get your body back. You're mentally and emotionally in a better place by this point in your journey and your body can take a hint. It realizes that it's time to align, stop fighting itself and function in the way it was intended.

Restore Your Possessions

An aspect of recovering from certain relationship wounds that's often overlooked is dealing with the loss of material possessions. After a bad breakup or divorce, for instance, many people lose sentimental items, homes, cars, clothing/jewelry, good credit or other possessions. Sometimes they were even destroyed. In this part of your journey, think of some of personal and material items you would like to restore. Of course, some things can never be replaced, but restore what you can. You will be surprised how powerful of an impact this one action can have on your healing process.

Restore Your Identity

Some wounds are so hurtful and shake your world so drastically that they make you question everything you thought you *knew*. When you experience *that* kind of wound, nothing seems certain anymore. It's to the point where you might even wonder whether the sky is, in fact, blue. But most devastatingly, you question what *you* knew about *you*. Your identity becomes a mystery. When you don't know who you are, it's impossible to figure out where you're supposed to be going. So the healing journey involves learning who you are again, or maybe even discovering yourself and your value for the first time.

Jesus restored.

After hanging on the cross for hours and feeling his natural life slip away from Him, you would have thought He was "losing" something. But instead, Luke 23:46 says that Jesus called out with a loud voice, **"Father, into Your hands I commit My spirit." When He had said this, He breathed His last.**[22] He **gave** his last breath and **gave** His spirit back to his Father. This was one of the most significant moments in history. By doing this, he restored the relationship between man and God. We regained access to eternal life with our Heavenly Father. Talk about a divine purpose!

So as you go through your healing journey…the overwhelming moments, the painful moments and even the doubtful moments, you are not alone. Even Jesus experienced every single one of those moments during His journey from betrayal to purpose. Remember, you can follow His excellent example and do the same thing in your own life.

CHAPTER NINE

Re-establishing

Peek into the Process

I decided I was going to walk through that door. If divine purpose was on the other side of it, I'd do whatever it took to get there. Healing just for the sake of going back to where my life was before "disruption" would have been okay. After all, my life was pretty good back then. But the truth is... I didn't want to settle for "pretty good." I wanted God's *best* for me. I longed to actually manifest the life and relationships I desired and deserved. Plus, I refused to let all that pain be in vain. I was going to cash the check I had earned through betrayal and brokenness. So I became strategic. I was committed to healing with intention and *establishing* a purpose-filled life.

Re-establishing began immediately after that cold January night when I'd sat on my couch with my blanket and YouTube. Needing the approval of people became a thing of the past. I refused to do *anything* that wasn't in alignment with what I believed was my purpose. I cut off certain relationships, disconnected from certain organizations and became laser-focused on what I called the *Produce Purpose Plan*, or *PPP*, that I'd created in order to implement it in my own life.

A couple weeks later, I started my graduate degree program so I could work towards my goal of being a decently-paid social worker. I took classes part-time and worked full-time at a company in the mental health field. I planned to get a couple of years under my belt there so when I finished my degree, I had the experience needed for promotion.

During this time, one of the other areas I began to put more focus on was my physical health. I had started exercising regularly and eating healthier. By this time my digestive system had stopped fighting me...thank goodness. I never realized how much I appreciated my stomach until "disruption" came.

Every major aspect of my life was addressed in my *Produce Purpose Plan*—career/professional, mental/emotional, spiritual, social, financial and physical. I started working the plan. But to my surprise, as I focused on re-establishing myself, God must have begun to work behind the scenes on someone else. Two months later, in March 2010, someone "new" inserted himself into my life. Now the interesting thing was he wasn't *totally* new. I had originally met him back in 2006, before "disruption." But we lived on two different continents and it had been years since I had heard from him. He was a guy I'd met during spring break in 2006 when I went on a mission trip to Sierra Leone, a small country in West Africa. He was the youth leader of the local church that my team had partnered with to do some mission work in his country. He handled some of the planning and coordination for our team. The most time that I'd personally spent with him was on the day I'd taught a dance to some of the Sierra Leonean youth. He had helped me find somewhere to plug in the little stereo I had so I could play the music for them.

After I returned from that trip, we exchanged a few simple "Hello, hope all is well," emails, but we hadn't exchanged any emails since early 2007, before my life had been uprooted.

So when he started reaching out to me regularly at the end of March 2010, showing a sudden intense interest in me, I was caught off guard…and curious.

We started chatting a few hours a day using *Yahoo* instant messenger. Then eventually we started talking via *Skype*. As I learned about this man, his values, his personality and his heart, I began to see that Prince coming into my life and at the time he came was a "purpose" thing. It was *supposed* to happen. If he would have come before "disruption" I wouldn't have really *seen* him. If he would have pursued me before doing the "work", I wouldn't have been so crystal clear on who I was and who I was supposed to connect to. Most notably, I wouldn't have been *whole*. Early on in our dating period, I realized Prince seemed to possess all the characteristics I wanted and needed in my future husband. Also, since we were continents apart, he clearly wasn't into me for sex. I needed to move very slowly in that area, so having the Atlantic Ocean between us definitely addressed that issue for me. But there was *one* thing that made me wonder whether God was playing a hilarious joke on me or if He just wanted to be sure I could catch a hint—that was his *name*. The man's given first name was *Prince*. "Seriously, God? Okay, I'm paying attention."

Prince and I decided to get serious after a few months of long-distance dating and made plans for a face-to-face visit. Prince decided to get a tourist visa to travel to America. But after submitting an application, paying an application fee and going to an in-person interview at the US Embassy in his country, he was denied the visa. No official reason was given, but Prince knew it was most likely based on the questions the embassy staff asked, because he was young and successful and they thought he was likely to overstay his visa. He wasn't immune to the stereotypes placed on immigrants from certain countries. That denial hit us hard. I'll never forget the phone conversation when he told me he was turned down for the tourist visa. He was in shock and having a hard time believing that a stranger sitting behind a desk had single-handedly shut down what we had spent months working toward. I didn't want to believe it, either.

Our relationship had hit a crossroad and all of a sudden I had a decision to make. If we were going to move forward with our relationship, I would need to travel back to Sierra Leone to visit *him*, instead. After a lot of prayer and reflecting on my life, our relationship and the phase of my healing journey I was in at the time, I came to the conclusion that I was supposed to go.

As I started to plan the trip, I let my close friends, mentors and family members know what was going on. As expected, I got plenty of opinions. Most were supportive and optimistic, because they knew me and trusted that I had done my homework. However, some of them thought I shouldn't go, that it was risky, and that it was just too "out there" to be what I was supposed to be doing. If I hadn't let go of my need to *please people* by this point, I would have listened to them. But it was too late. I had learned how to listen to my own voice, tune into my own heart, and focus on doing what I felt God wanted me to do...regardless of what "they" had to say. "They" meant well but "they" no longer controlled what I did or how I thought about myself. During my healing process, I had learned to tune "them" out.

Prince and I continued to develop our relationship and we grew closer and closer. We would chat at least four to five hours every day and do a video call almost every night. We had "virtual dates" like watching movies together. We would actually countdown and press play together so it'd feel like we were watching it together. We even picked a book to read about courtship and preparing for marriage and I sent him a physical copy so we could read it together. We did what it took to stay connected and build a strong relationship despite the huge distance between us.

Since I was in graduate school and would need to take my vacation in-between semesters, I planned for my trip to take place during the Christmas break. So it was settled. In three months, the same two close friends who were at my side in court that day with my rapist would travel with me to Sierra Leone to meet my Prince. I literally saw my life coming full circle. *Re-establishing* was in full effect.

When you decided to be intentional about healing your heart after brokenness, it was because you wanted to heal, but it was also because you didn't want that situation to define you. You still wanted the life and relationships you deserve and you were willing to put in the work to do it. Well, that's the purpose of *Re-establishing*. This is the step of the healing journey where you should shift from *intention* to *action* and become strategic in your personal life so you can begin manifesting the things you desire. I think it's important that I share what I mean when I use the term *manifest*. I define *manifestation* as simply, "when a belief becomes real." We are always manifesting things in our lives, whether positive or negative, because we're always *thinking*. This is an undeniable reality—because our thoughts become beliefs, our beliefs determine our behaviors/decisions, and our behaviors/decisions manifest outcomes. And if you'd like to manifest the type of life you desire in every area— career/professional, mental/emotional, spiritual, social, financial and physical—you have to do some *Re-establishing*.

Now that you're clear about why you want to experience *Re-establishing*, I want to explain what it takes to experience it based on the **Heal Intentionally Blueprint©**:

Re-establish Boundaries

Boundaries are important. They also serve multiple purposes. One of them is to keep certain people and things out of a particular space or place. When you experienced a personal violation and were wounded by someone you trusted, your boundaries were crossed. A huge part of your healing process is re-establishing your boundaries in order to protect yourself and guard your heart in the future. Speaking of boundaries, many women struggle with using one particular two-letter word, "No," in order to avoid hurting people's feelings, not to appear mean or unkind, or sometimes because they've used the word *No* in the past but someone chose to ignore it and violated them. I understand all of these reasons at a personal level. However, part of choosing yourself is deciding to fall in love with the word *No*, valuing it, and using it whenever necessary.

Another purpose boundaries serve is to prevent you from drifting too far off and finding yourself outside of where you belong. And in this case, the place you "belong" is in *purpose*. Sometimes people, "stuff", money or circumstances can serve as distractions and pull you outside of your purpose. When you are called to *significance*, which you are, there will be situations and circumstances that happen in your life meant to take you off your course and abort your destiny. It's probably already happened to you in the past, which is why you're reading this book. Part of your job now is to re-establish and strengthen your boundaries to not only keep certain stuff out, but also to make sure you stay in your place of purpose.

Re-establish Routines

According to Oxford Dictionaries, a routine is "a sequence of actions regularly followed."[23] When you experience a relationship wound, it usually uproots and throws many of your routines out of whack. "Regular" and "normal" aren't a part of your vocabulary for a while. This is because how, where and with whom you "did" life may have drastically changed as a result of that wound. For example, routines around where you lived, worked or worshiped, how you celebrated holidays/traditions or even the everyday tasks in your life may look different now. They may have even ceased to exist. This is a shock to the system in the early weeks and months after *disruption*. However, in the *Re-establishing* step of your journey, you *intentionally* **use *routine*** in order to manifest the life you desire.

In order to manifest the life you desire and crush the value out of the violation you experienced, you have to re-establish a **routine** for every area of your life. This is what the *Produce Purpose Plan* did for me. First you'll need to create and implement a self-care routine that prioritizes your mental and emotional health. Self-care can no longer be something you do *if* you have time. Instead, it must become something you *always* do because it *creates* more time to do everything else. People who don't practice self-care can unknowingly waste a lot time making mistakes due to overwhelm, staying stuck due to constant worry and fail to step into what is possible for them due to constantly questioning their worth. Don't let this be you. Open yourself up to be honored by others by first honoring yourself. You may have been broken, but again, it did not diminish your value. You deserve to be cherished and cared for but you can't solely depend on others to do so. So remember to "plant your own gardens and decorate your own soul, instead of waiting for someone to bring you flowers."[24]

When it comes to your spiritual health, develop a regular practice that emphasizes silence and listening intently, prayer and reading scripture, as well as regular connection with people who encourage and equip you to grow in your faith. Doing this will build you the strong foundation you need to handle the shifts and changes which will definitely come your way. Keep in mind that as important as it is to seek depth in God and be intentional about your life, make sure you're not so deep and serious that you forget to have some fun! As human beings, we actually have a need for fun as well as a need for connection with others. So yes… make sure to fit a social life and some silliness into your schedule.

When you implement these routines in a consistent way you'll begin to peel away layers and levels of impact the relationship wound(s) may have had on your life. For example, sometimes survivors of abusive relationships or people who've recently divorced don't realize the impact their relationship had on their financial lives until *this* point of their journey. As they begin to re-establish themselves in this area by taking a look at unpaid debts or their credit report, many times they are completely shocked at the damage. Financial wounds are a real thing. Creating a routine to slowly but steadily take back your finances is an important part of your process and you cannot minimize the positive impact it will have on your life.

When it comes to your career or profession, start a routine that pushes you closer to your ultimate goals. Whether it's learning a new skill, networking with people in the industry, or returning to school, it's important to have a plan and consistently work it.

Lastly, creating a routine around your physical health is essential. When something is off with your body, it can negatively impact whatever else you're trying to do. Not feeling well or not having the energy you need to do everything you want to do can be frustrating and discouraging. So when you're in a season of re-establishing yourself, be sure to keep yourself well-nourished and equipped for the work being done by eating well, exercising regularly and listening to your body. Doing this will make sure you're fit for your journey.

Re-establish Relationships

As I mentioned at the very beginning of this book, at our very core, human beings are relational. We need relationships to thrive and when we're healthy, we desire them. But when you've been traumatized by someone you trusted, you can lose that desire and have trouble pushing past the fear of being hurt again. The good news is that if you follow the steps outlined in the **Heal Intentionally Blueprint©**, you will release fear and restore your desire to pursue your purpose, despite the pain you've experienced. During *Re-establishing* you intentionally begin rebuilding every area your life—which includes your relationships.

The most important relationship to re-establish is actually the relationship you have with yourself. Honoring yourself with radical self-care, making sure your basic human needs are being met and prioritizing your own desires is the formula for becoming the best version of you. When we become the best version of ourselves, by default we will manifest the life and relationships we desire.

It's during this part of your journey that you may be ready to accept a new intimate relationship in your life, open yourself up to the idea of a new close friendship or join that new church. Whatever your relationship wound was, you're ready to reclaim that particular area of your life. To go back to the boxing analogy, during this step in your journey you're ready to go back in for another "round." Remember at the beginning of the book when we talked about you being like a boxer who got knocked out? Well, it's during this step of the journey that you feel strong enough to come out of your corner and get back into the fight, knowing you've healed and you're stronger now. Now you *know* that you'll win in the end.

When you experienced hurt and betrayal, that person did something which impacted your life because they had *influence* in your life. In almost all relationships, the other person has some level of influence over you and your life. That's the nature of relationships. However, when there is relationship trauma, that person takes advantage of their influence or role in the relationship and violates or betrays the other person in the relationship. So whether your relationship wound came from a close friend, family member, partner, spouse, mentor, spiritual leader or a toxic co-worker or boss...it's during this step that you face the very area in which you were hurt and reintroduce relationship back into your life. And because you've healed intentionally, by this point in your journey, you're whole enough to experience relationships fully and equipped enough to balance *giving* your heart, *nurturing* your heart and *guarding* your heart. Most importantly, you know pursuing that balance must become part of your daily routine.

The overall purpose of *Re-establishing* is to serve as building, training and preparation ground for the next season of your life. It calls on you to build things as you go without knowing everything about the final product. It encourages you to keep pushing and stay committed to doing your routines, even when it gets hard and you don't see immediate results. And through daily decisions made consistently over time, such as implementing your self-care routine, praying and studying regularly, taking on new challenges at work or in your business or re-establishing healthy relationships while maintaining your boundaries, you prepare yourself to manifest the life and relationships you desire.

Jesus re-established.

After an excruciating death on the cross, Jesus was buried in a tomb. But after three days He arose, and when He did, He immediately began *Re-establishing* a few things. During the forty days that the risen Jesus walked the earth, He re-established His relationships with the disciples, which built their faith.[25] The Bible goes on to mention that He also re-established His *routine* of teaching the scriptures, sharing about the Kingdom, and loving on people.[26] He did this to be sure the disciples were equipped to do what they were called to do in Matthew 28:18-20, which was to:

"Therefore go and make disciples of all nations, baptizing them in the name of the Father and of the Son and of the Holy Spirit, and teaching them to obey everything I have commanded you. And surely I am with you always, to the very end of the age."

That scripture tells us what Jesus ultimately wanted to re-establish...the church. And by church, He wasn't talking about a brick building with four walls, a preacher and a pulpit. He was talking about you and me. He wanted you to be saved and live your best life. He knew you would have struggles and experience pain and disappointment, but he wanted you to be able access true healing. He knew you would have moments where you questioned your worth, but He wanted you to know He sacrificed His life just for you. He did all of this on purpose and for purpose. He accepted His purpose and was laser-focused on accomplishing it so ultimately *you* could accomplish yours.

Re-establishing is an amazing part of your journey. If you do the work of the previous steps, you'll be ready to experience the explosion of energy, passion and purpose that comes with it. You've got this. Be willing to do the work. Be willing to sacrifice *certainty* for *significance*. Settling is safe but *significance*, which is purposeful, intentional and dependent on knowing who and Whose you are, is what brings true success. When you live fully aware of your significance, no matter what disruption or distraction comes your way, you will be able to heal, find the value in the violation and eventually *Redeem* what you desire and deserve.

> *Be willing to sacrifice certainty for significance.*

CHAPTER TEN

Redeeming

Peek into the Process

Re-establishing didn't happen overnight. It was one of the most challenging and intense yet rewarding years of my life. It helped to build my endurance, my faith and my resolve. It required a combination of working, waiting, believing and building toward something I had seen glimpses of but not a crystal clear picture. However, the future is *never* crystal clear until it becomes the present. In the meantime, I had to be content with glimpses and rely on faith until I got there. I had no idea how long *Re-establishing* would last, and because I didn't know the timing, it required me to balance staying present in the moment while also pressing toward the mark. It was a delicate dance which strengthened my character but truly tested my endurance.

But as I sat there in a chair, *this* time surrounded by my bridesmaids and wearing my beautiful white wedding gown, I realized I was **Redeeming**. As I glanced down at my engagement ring, my mind drifted back to a year earlier when Prince had placed the ring on my finger during my trip back to Sierra Leone.

Throughout the visit, I watched him with both my natural and my spiritual eyes. So much of our relationship had been by faith, but I finally had a chance to use my sight! And if I'm honest, my touch too! Good Lord! I hadn't had the opportunity to hold hands with or kiss the man that I loved. It was nice to reach out and touch this very *real* man with whom I'd spent so many months talking via electronic device for hours on end. This tall, handsome, intelligent African man was *my* man. I hadn't been able to show him off to my friends and family and we hadn't even been able to go on *actual* dates, so in so many ways our relationship hadn't been a "normal" relationship. Then again, I wasn't "normal" either…another reality this journey helped me to not only accept, but which now I embraced. I wasn't "normal." But I also wasn't called to be "normal."

So yes, I watched him. For instance, I watched him do everything necessary to make sure my vision for a girls conference where I would also have a chance to teach and mentor one hundred girls while we were there came to pass…from location, to attendees, to support staff and sound. He was on top of it all. It gave me confidence that he would always be a VIP on my team and support whatever I was doing, if we were to do life together. I watched him insist on and pay for all of our lodging, food, transportation and entertainment while we were there despite us being the ones from the wealthiest nation in the world. So I knew he could be a provider. I watched as he interacted with his family, his friends, my friends and even strangers on the street. His reserved nature and his quiet, yet confident disposition gave me a sense of predictability and safety…something I knew I would need. But his humility revealed the most to me about his character. He was *that guy*. The guy everyone respected, wanted to be connected to and held in high regard, yet he was one of the most gracious and humble men I had ever met. This gave me assurance that he could handle a woman like me who knows who she is and uses her voice, but not see that as a threat to his ego.

On one of the last few days of our trip, Prince took me and my friends to Aberdeen beach, a tourist beach right off the coast of Africa. It was so beautiful. The beach-style restaurants, Atlantic Ocean water and countless grains of sand on the shore of the Mother Land were a lot to take in. While we were walking along the beach, Prince suddenly stopped and got on one knee. He grabbed my hand and asked if I would allow him to spend his life with me. I said "Yes!" and then he placed this beautiful engagement ring on my finger.

I lifted my eyes away from my ring and back to the note card I was holding in that same hand. The note card had my wedding vows written on it and as I started reading them again, I became a little emotional. Just downstairs, in about forty-five minutes, I'd actually be reciting my vows. Getting from the engagement to the altar wasn't as simple as it is for most couples. I remembered the anxious patience we'd experienced going through the intimidating months-long immigration process required in order to get married and live in the US, which we had decided to do. Although we knew our future was technically dependent on immigration officials and properly filed paperwork, we ultimately depended on what God had said about our future. And finally, after a year of working, waiting, believing and building toward something we couldn't know for sure would even happen, but that we trusted and believed was part of our purpose, we were only moments away from saying, "I do."

So I just sat there ... frozen again, but *this* time it was because I was overwhelmed with joy and sheer gratitude for my journey. I was healed and whole, my pain had been turned into purpose and I'd somehow found the beauty in all that betrayal.

I had been raped twice…but was still a virgin. My wedding night still had a special significance to me. As a result of the

> *I had been raped twice…but was still a virgin.*

healing journey I'd walked through, I knew that my value was still intact. My value was something I had to *give*, it could not be something *taken* by means of violation. I looked forward to actually *giving* my body to a man for the first time. Although I would have rather not experienced the wounds at all, I was thankful for the journey of healing from them and grateful for the woman I'd become…in part, because of them, and in part, in spite of them.

What are you looking forward to *Redeeming*? What would you like to recover? Are you willing to use the power of routine and create unique systems in your life that when implemented will manifest the outcomes you desire? If so, you will eventually reach this phase of your healing journey where you'll begin to receive beauty for your ashes.[27] That which was harmful and toxic, you'll exchange for something of value which adds to your life.

To be clear, I'm not saying that everyone will win the lottery, meet their husband and find a new car in their driveway when they reach this step in the journey. *Redeeming* will look different for every person. Some people will redeem a healthier body and feel full of life for the first time in a long time. Some people will redeem a level of self-esteem they hadn't had since childhood. Some people will redeem new opportunities in their business or promotion on their job. Some people will redeem relationships that had been broken, or form completely new ones with people who are in alignment with your purpose and values. Although you may not know when it will happen or how it will look, trust that you will reach this part of your journey. *Redeeming* is the final destination of a journey that starts with pain, proceeds through a process and eventually reaches purpose.

In this final step you can expect to:

Redeem What You Lost

The time you lost, the joy you lost, the confidence you lost, the stuff you lost, the relationships you lost, even the hope you lost will be redeemed. I also want to acknowledge those of you reading who think you lost your value when you were use, abused, or violated in some way. You didn't. By now, I hope you are open to redeem even what you *thought* you lost, but really never did. In this stage of your journey expect to receive and expect to recover. And how the whole divine purpose thing works is that what you redeem may be worth even more than what was lost or stolen through violation.

Redeem What You Desire

We all have desires we hope for. However, when you decide to heal intentionally, you go a step beyond *hoping* for your desires and commit to *healing* for your desires. Healing for your desires serves as evidence of preparation to receive them. So if you have gotten to this stage in your journey, expect to begin to see the manifestation of things you've desired for your life. Expect to see some of your beliefs become real.

Redeem What You Deserve

In *Redeeming* there will be some circumstances, people and opportunities which come into your life that you didn't know you wanted and had no idea you needed. There will be amazing things which come your way that you didn't really expect or desire but that come your way because they're things you *deserve.* In other words, they're things you've earned. You've had to invest tears and time into brokenness, but because you went through the process of healing intentionally, brokenness didn't diminish your value— it increased it. So in this stage of your journey you can expect a return on your investment.

Jesus was redeemed.

He had been betrayed by a trusted friend, been beaten, bruised and hung to die on a cross, and then rose from the dead. Through His sacrifice, He re-established our relationship to the Creator of Heaven and Earth. Jesus had indeed turned His pain into purpose.

He had spent forty days teaching and building up the disciples so they could re-establish the church when He left. Then scripture says **"Jesus led them outside the city, blessed them and "was taken up into heaven and He sat at the right hand of God."**[28] It was in that moment He was finally able to reclaim His rightful position sitting next to His Father in heaven. Now finally, He too had been redeemed.

I'm not sure where you are in your journey right now. When you began reading this book you could have been at the beginning, still *Reeling*, or perhaps you were somewhere in the middle, around *Reviewing* or *Releasing*. It could be that when you started this book you thought you had finished all your healing work, but now you realize there are a few steps in the **Heal Intentionally Blueprint©** that you skipped or didn't realize you still needed to make. Or perhaps it's been a while since your wound happened and you're doing pretty good, but like me, you don't want to settle for "pretty good." Instead, you prefer God's *best* and to manifest the life and relationships you desire and deserve. If you fit into any of those categories, I encourage you to read on to the last section of the book.

In Part Three, DISCHARGE, you'll learn how to craft your own *Heal Intentionally Discharge Plan*. People don't plan to fail, they fail to plan.[29] When you leave the hospital or outpatient clinic following surgery, you are given a discharge plan. The discharge plan includes instructions on how to take care of yourself at home, prescription medications to fill, people and places to go for follow-up care, as well as symptoms to look out for that could mean you're not healing well, are developing an infection or having a setback. If you do that to make sure you heal after undergoing treatment for a physical illness or wound, why wouldn't you do the same after healing from a relationship wound?

The purpose of the *Heal Intentionally Discharge Plan* is to help you *stay* whole and stay healed after you complete the **Heal Intentionally Blueprint©**. In other words, it will help you *maintain* your healing. Maintenance is one of the most important yet neglected aspects of the healing process. But failing to do regular maintenance in your life when you've experienced a serious relationship wound is very risky, because you could find yourself blindsided and broken down again. Life is full of surprises, and we can't control everything or everyone who comes our way. You never know when the next toxic person will come drifting into your life. Not only that, but when you live a purpose-filled life instead of being content with mediocrity, you may attract people who will make it their mission to take from you, break you, slander you or seek to use you for their own selfish ends. All of these reasons explain why having a discharge plan is so important. It will serve as something to guide you, protect you and maintain you, but also will warn you if you unintentionally drift into a toxic or unhealthy relationship or environment, so you won't stay there a second longer than necessary.

With that said, let's talk discharge planning...

PART THREE

Discharge

CHAPTER ELEVEN

Craft Your Plan

When I was a medical social worker, I read, created and coordinated my fair share of patient discharge plans. Discharge planning is important because studies have shown a well-crafted and well-implemented discharge plan reduces the likelihood of a patient being readmitted to the hospital or developing complications.[30] Although the types of wounds we've been discussing are relationship wounds, a universal life principle still applies. That principle is when you have a good plan, and then do what it takes to implement it, you increase the likelihood of long-term success. The *Heal Intentionally Discharge Plan* is meant to be your tool that helps you do just that.

If you're reading right now and you are still somewhere on the path to complete healing, let this discharge plan motivate you to stay committed to your journey. You will get here. And since you've read this book and now know what you need to do get here, your chances of complete recovery just went through the roof. In the next and final chapter, where I'll wrap up, I'll give you some pointed advice on how to keep pursuing your health, as well as how I could possibly partner with you on your journey. So keep reading!

Your *Heal Intentionally Discharge Plan* will help you to address three key areas to maintaining your health after recovering from a relationship wound. Let's go through each of them one by one…

Take Your Prescription

Think about this part of your discharge plan as your *medication regimen*. When a doctor prescribes a medication, it's meant to either improve your body's performance of a certain function, like a vitamin or supplement, or its purpose is to prevent a particular symptom that could negatively impact you. For example, a blood pressure medication is prescribed to prevent a heart attack.

Well, for the maintenance of your relationship wound, there are certain things you'll need to implement daily into your life and certain ones which are good to do on an as-needed basis. You've actually already heard of the "medication" and are familiar with the effects. That's because in order to maintain your healing and continue to manifest the life and relationships you desire, the prescriptions you need to take are actually steps of the **Heal Intentionally Blueprint©**. Here's your prescription…

Take the following daily:

Resting - Check in with yourself daily. Be sure to practice mindfulness and gratitude. Prioritize your spirituality and self-care. Take care of your body. Be intentional about sitting in silence every now and then and allow your emotions to inform you but not to dictate to you.

Receiving - Be sure to keep your glass full or at least do everything you can to make sure it doesn't get empty. Avoid the trap of becoming everything for everybody else while failing to receive what you need to what you need for yourself. Yes, you do have needs and yes, you deserve some of your wants. Allow others of your choosing to encourage, support, teach and inspire you.

Re-establishing - Develop and implement daily routines for every area of your life—career/professional, mental/emotional, spiritual, social, financial and physical. Make sure you create healthy habits for your life that will continue to push you toward purpose. It will also prevent you from drifting too far off from where you want to be. Make goal-setting a regular practice and update your routines as you reach goals you've set yourself.

Take the following as needed (PRN):

Releasing- Although this may not be a daily issue, if you begin to experience certain unwanted or negative emotions due to life circumstances, remember to release any G.A.S. or resentment on an as-needed basis. Also, whenever you realize someone has come into your life who is not supposed to be there, feel free to release them. Lastly, if you find yourself in a job, situation or circumstance that doesn't feel quite right or is not in alignment with your values, feel free to release yourself from it as soon as the need arises.

Reviewing - Every once in a while, but especially after any major life event, whether positive or negative, don't forget to do a *review*. Use the opportunity to take note of your thoughts and beliefs about the life event, situation or circumstance and decide which ones you want to keep and which to throw away. *Reviewing* regularly will ensure that you don't carry unhealthy and unhelpful beliefs in your heart and mind for years before you even notice. This particular medication serves a preventative purpose. You may not see results right away, but the long-term impact is undeniable.

Disclaimer: Results of these medications will vary but you can expect to see decreased *Reeling* and an increase in *Restoring* and *Redeeming*.

Avoid an Infection

One of the biggest risk factors for complications after receiving any treatment is the possibility of developing an infection. Infections are most likely to happen when recently treated patients have a weak immune system, are exposed to an unclean environment for too long and bacteria or a virus gains unhindered access to the wound, or if the person who experienced the wound fails to practice proper hygiene.

These are the same risk factors you have to avoid after you've experienced a relationship wound. In order to make sure you stay healthy and avoid repeat wound issues, take the following precautions:

Immunity

Your immune system is your biggest defense against any illness, infection or disease in your body. Well, when it comes building your immunity in a "life" sense, it means intentionally doing activities that strengthen your defense against distraction, drama and poor decision-making. One sure way to build your immunity from all of those is to stay connected to God and tuned in to His voice.

Also, having a system or routine like the *Produce Purpose Plan* I outlined in *Re-establishing* will help you stay focused and decrease distraction. The best way to avoid drama is to avoid gossip and be selective with who is in your inner circle.

However, your decisions pack the most power when it comes to defense. If we are honest, every single aspect of our lives, past and present, are the direct result of our decisions. Because even when life happens to us and it's outside of our control, we still decide how we will respond to it. Building immunity against poor-decision making will be your greatest defense against anything that could hinder your growth or try to derail your purpose. Improving in this area is the result of gaining wisdom, slaying fear and becoming someone who can take quick but inspired action.

Environment

There's a famous quote that says "You are a product of your environment."[31] Your environment *will* affect you, whether it's in a good way or a not-so-good way. Due to this reality, being intentional about the spaces and places we spend our lives in is not *optional*. This is especially true when you've experienced serious relationship wounds or traumatic experiences in your life. The truth is, those wounds, especially if they're more recent, can cause you to be vulnerable to sharks who seek out prey and know how to find the person in the room who's been recently wounded.

For that reason and many others, your discharge plan recommends that you seek "controlled environments" as much as possible. To accomplish this, try to avoid toxic, unhealthy or otherwise unsanitary spaces at all costs. And if you *have* to go into an environment in which you typically wouldn't prefer to be because it's work or family-related, make sure you manage your time there and don't stay too long. Similar to a wound left in an unclean environment for too long becoming susceptible to infection, so too are you susceptible to infection if you stay in a toxic environment for too long.

Hygiene

Hygiene is the practice of taking care of yourself. After undergoing surgery, many patients are left with a wound. The wound may involve surgical stitches, glue stitches, packing the wound, the need to apply medication to it and/or the need to bandage it. Wound care is a huge component of recovery after a treatment or procedure. It's important that patients clean and care for their wounds as instructed or else they risk the wounds becoming infected. An infected wound can cause a setback in the patient's recovery, create new painful symptoms or even land them back in the hospital.

Hygiene is also an important part of recovering from relationship wounds. The means by which we take care of ourselves are through deliberate, intentional and sometimes radical self-care. Self-care isn't just going to get a pedicure or a massage every couple of weeks. It's so much more than that. Truly experiencing the positive effects of genuine self-care requires a mindset shift. First, accept the notion that self-care isn't just a suggestion, but a requirement. Second, embrace the knowledge that you deserve radical self-care and are worth it. Third, acknowledge the fact that you cannot be any good to anyone if you're not first kind to yourself. Self-care is a critical element of your discharge plan and should not be taken lightly.

Watch for Red Flags

One of the most important parts of a discharge plan is where it lists the Red Flags. They're usually found on the final page and typed in big and bold letters so they're not easy to miss. Red flags are the signs or symptoms which require immediate action if you begin experiencing them. They could mean you're experiencing a complication, negative side effects or developing an infection.

The recovery process from a relationship wound involves you doing everything you can to recognize Red Flags when you see them and take immediate action. Here are some Red Flags to keep an eye out for as you strive to maintain your healing:

Discomfort

Discomfort manifests as pain, restlessness, irritability or just not feeling like yourself. If you notice this, it could mean that there is something or someone in your life who has breached your boundaries. You'll need to take action to find out who or what it is and quickly remove it or them.

Weakness

You may experience weakness due to feeling like you don't have control over yourself or your environment, or if someone in your life begins to exhibit controlling behaviors. This Red Flag also means that immediate action is required. Enlist the help of a trusted mentor or friend to encourage you or give you strategy to regain your sense of control.

Lethargy

This could look like a sudden lack of energy or lost desire to pursue your purpose and goals for your life. This could be the result of discouragement or stagnation. Implement your *routines* and ramp of your self-care to jolt yourself out of that space. Its okay to rest, but it's important that you don't get complacent.

Insomnia

Insomnia, which is chronic difficulty or inability to sleep, can make it difficult to think, focus, and even function. If you begin to have difficulty resting your heart, mind, body or spirit due to stress or recent life circumstances, it's a sign that your life needs some extra attention.

If you notice any of these Fed Flags in your life, address them quickly and avoid letting them fester. Keep your recovery on track and continue to manifest the life and relationships you desire and deserve.

So that's the make-up of the *Heal Intentionally Discharge Plan*. It's a practical and powerful tool to use in order to be intentional about staying healed and staying whole. If you're interested in taking the content you've read in this book and truly applying it to your life in a more tangible way, I would love to support you and give you the opportunity to do that.

There's a saying that says all good things must come to an end. But I don't want that to be the case with our relationship. If you've read this entire book, you know me pretty darn well! We're connected now! I've really enjoyed writing this book, sharing my story with you, and hopefully inspiring you to truly embrace your story, as well. Now I ask that you turn the page one last time so I can share some final thoughts with you and also let you know how we can stay connected…

CONCLUSION

Pursue Your Healing

So what's next for you?

Now you know how to heal intentionally, turn your pain into purpose, and discover the beauty in betrayal. So if you're wondering what the next step is, the answer is **PURSUE**. It's time to pursue your healing. Information alone is great but many times it doesn't change us. However, when we add information and application together, now that is the recipe for transformation.

Writing such a transparent and personal book was a challenge for me. It really stretched me. And honestly, it was a little scary. Okay, a lot scary. Anyone who knows me personally knows that by nature, I'm a deeply private person. But *you* were so important to me that I pushed past myself, so I could get to you. Yes, *you*... the amazing person reading this book. I have a special place in my heart for people who have experienced a wound when they had their guard down…or who have been traumatized by someone they were supposed to be able to trust. I've come to realize that it is my life's work to share the ***Heal Intentionally Blueprint*©** with the world as a solution to this all-too-common experience. There is a way to move past the pain of betrayal. But you can't go around it, above it, or beneath it…you must go *through* it. That's because through it is how you find the path to purpose.

So where are you within the 8-Step Journey? Where were you before you picked up this book? Reeling? Releasing? Re-establishing? If you haven't taken a moment to think about the answer to that question yet, do you mind doing that now? Feel free to take a glance back at the *Table of Contents* if it helps…

The reason I asked you to think about where you are in your healing process is because if you answered that question with any step/phase other than "Discharge," or "Craft Your Plan," there is potential for even greater healing and greater levels of purpose. And even if you've reached "Discharge," sometimes it's beneficial to "loop back" to previous phases of the journey to experience even deeper levels of healing.[32]

The point I want to leave with you is to PURSUE. Pursue your healing, pursue your purpose and pursue the life and relationships you desire and deserve.

It has been such an honor to walk with you through the pages of this book. It's my hope that you refer to it whenever you need a reminder of your value and a word of encouragement to keep being intentional as you move forward in your journey.

I invite you to go to a special page on my website just for my book readers. I mentioned it earlier in the book, but just in case you forgot, head over to **www.valueinviolation.com/bonuses** to get your book bonuses.

Whenever I'm about to end a coaching session or call with a client, I like to ask them about their takeaways. So I'm curious, what's been most helpful or insightful from *The Value in Violation*? What's the meaningful action you plan to take after reading the book? I'd really love to hear your answers! Feel free to share them with me by email by sending it to coach@ chaenahollist.com. I would love to reach as many people as possible with the **Heal Intentionally** message. So if this book was helpful to you, would you mind letting others know by recommending it to a friend who you know could use some encouragement or by leaving a book review on Amazon? I would be so grateful.

Well this doesn't have to be goodbye. I prefer the end of this book to be the beginning of our partnership on this journey of life and purpose! You can connect with me on social media @CoachChaena on Facebook and @ChaenaHollist on Instagram, Twitter, and Periscope. But the absolute best way to make sure we stay connected and don't miss one another due to crowded nature of social media, visit my internet home at **www.chaenahollist.com** and subscribe to my email inner circle. When you subscribe, you'll receive a free gift from me as well as regular emails with encouragement and tools to help you on your journey.

It's been an honor sharing time with you and holding space for you as we walked through this journey together. I will be eternally grateful for that gift.

Sending love and gratitude from my heart to yours.

~ Chaena

P.S. Now Pursue!!

APPENDIX A

Value in Violation Academy

Congratulations! You've invested in yourself and your purpose by reading this book. Your future is worth it.

The book website (www.valueinviolation.com) has plenty of extra tools and bonus content to help you on your journey to *Heal Intentionally*. While you're there, be sure to join our tribe and connect to other people who are on the same journey you're on.

If you'd like additional guidance, mentoring, and support as you determine where you are within the Heal Intentionally Blueprint, create your personalized Produce Purpose Plan, and craft your Heal Intentionally Discharge Plan—I'M IN.

I created a program that is perfect for people who want to take the content they've learned in this book and apply it to their lives in a more tangible way. It's called **Value in Violation Academy**.

The purpose of the program is very clear—equip you to heal intentionally and manifest the life and relationships you desire.

Value in Violation Academy is available as a self-study online course as well as a more in-depth and powerful group coaching experience that includes personal coaching from me.

Together we'll develop your plan to heal *on* purpose and *for* purpose. Together we'll ensure that your wounds won't win … you will.

To get more information about Value in Violation Academy, go to www.valueinviolation.com

Become Certified in the Heal Intentionally Blueprint

For Coaches, Counselors, Leaders and Professionals

The message of Heal Intentionally is BIGGER than me.

I'm not keeping it to myself. I'd like some help sharing this blueprint for hope and healing.

If you or your organization serves and works with people who've experienced relationship wounds and desire to help them heal intentionally, turn their pain into purpose and find beauty after betrayal, consider becoming certified in the Heal Intentionally Blueprint.

Continue to walk in your purpose but add the Heal Intentionally Blueprint to YOUR toolbox.

FIND OUT MORE AT
www.valueinviolation.com

BRING CHAENA TO YOUR EVENT OR ORGANIZATION

Chaena knows the power of the spoken word as a catalyst for change and transformation in people. Choosing the right speaker for your event is an important decision. Chaena's servant-leader approach to speaking combined with her powerful content positions her as a great choice for groups and organizations that resonate with her message of hope and healing. Chaena approaches each opportunity to speak as a unique assignment by tailoring her message or training to meet and exceed the goals of her clients.

CONTACT CHAENA TODAY TO BEGIN THE CONVERSATION
www.chaenahollist.com

Acknowledgments

Writing this book was one of the most difficult and rewarding experiences of my life. It took me out of my comfort zone and required me to reach back into some of the most painful seasons of my life. However, it changed my life. I'm a different and better woman, wife, mother, friend, entrepreneur, teacher and coach as a result. I will be forever grateful for the book writing process and it wouldn't have been possible without my dream team...

To God...thank you for always being strength in my weakness and for saving me by your limitless grace.

To my husband, Prince, you are my partner and best friend, and I'm so grateful for the blessing of doing life with you. Thank you for never complaining about the many nights I stayed up late working on this book and for trying your best to keep our five year old and two year old from disturbing me too much...although most of the time it didn't work despite your best efforts! I love you honey.

Speaking of my two children, Chanice and Prince II, you are my energy and my joy. Thank you for just being you.

To my parents, Karla and Sam Fleming, as well as my siblings Leigh, Sam and Cameron, you have always been in my corner. I will love you always.

To my friends who held me down and supported my book journey by simply being there: Ashley Banks, Karissa Haugabook, Judah Haugabook, Tiffany Mitchell, Timothy Mitchell, Tameka Lewis, and Tiesha White ... Thank you!

To my entrepreneurial mentors, personal and spiritual mentors, and coaches: Rosetta Thurman, Tiphani Montgomery, Kary Oberbrunner, Debra Carr, Dr. Regina Spellmon, Bishop Kevin Dickerson and Pastor Sonjia Dickerson, your influence on my life has been invaluable and the seeds of wisdom and guidance that you planted have resulted in this project. I will be forever grateful.

And to you, my readers, as well as my clients, past, present, and future, you are my inspiration and my motivation for it all. It's my hope that this book encouraged, equipped, and strengthened you on your journey. Thank you for allowing me to be your teacher ... and thank you for continuing to teach me.

About the Author

Chaena Hollist, LMSW is a licensed master social worker, minister, personal growth strategist, and speaker committed to decreasing the number of people walking around wounded in the world.

As a transformational teacher and mentor, Chaena helps people *heal intentionally* after brokenness and betrayal so they can manifest the life and relationships they desire and deserve. Her clients appreciate her personable and practical approach to helping them extract wisdom from their wounds and passionately pursue their purpose.

Chaena is a graduate of the University of Texas at Arlington where she earned a Bachelor's of Social Work as well as a Master of Science in Social Work. She also has many years of professional experience in the fields of mental health and trauma recovery.

As a survivor of sexual abuse as a child and acquaintance rape as a young adult, Chaena knows firsthand how it feels to walk around wounded in the fog of betrayal. Today, a transformed woman, she has a passion to help other people reclaim their significance and reach their highest potential.

Chaena loves to sing and snuggle up for a good television show. She strives to live a lifestyle focused on creating impact and creating memories. Her favorite memories to create are ones that involve her husband and best friend, Prince Hollist, and their two beautiful children.

Connect at www.ChaenaHollist.com

VIVA

Value in Violation Academy

THE PURPOSE:

Equip you to heal intentionally and manifest the life and relationships you desire.

VALUE IN VIOLATION ACADEMY WILL HELP YOU:

- Pinpoint where you are on your "Heal Intentionally" journey
- Create your personalized Produce Purpose Plan
- Craft your customized Heal Intentionally Discharge Plan

Let me help you on your journey to turn your Pain into Purpose.

Value in Violation Academy is available as a self-study online course and as a powerful group coaching experience.

If you're interested in PURSUING your next step, I want to support you.

VISIT
ValueInViolation.com

Endnotes

[1] Widom, Cathy Spatz, Sally J Czaja, and Mary Ann Dutton. "Childhood Victimization and Lifetime Revictimization." *Child abuse & neglect* 32, no. 8 (2008): 785-96.

[2] Biello, David. "What Is a Medically Induced Coma and Why Is It Used." https://www.scientificamerican.com/article/what-is-a-medically-induced-coma/

[3] Pietrangelo, Ann, and Stephanie Watson. "The Effects of Sleep Deprivation on Your Body." Healthline. https://www.health-line.com/health/sleep-deprivation/effects-on-body#1 (accessed August 5, 2018).

[4] Beris, Rebecca. "Science Says Silence Is Much More Important To Our Brains Than We Think." Lifehack. https://www.life-hack.org/377243/science-says-silence-much-more-important-our-brains-than-thought (accessed August 5, 2018).

[5] Mccraty, Rollin, and Maria A. Zayas. "Cardiac Coherence, Self-regulation, Autonomic Stability, and Psychosocial Well-being." Frontiers in Psychology 5 (2014). Accessed August 5, 2018. doi:10.3389/fpsyg.2014.01090.

6   Mccraty, Rollin, and Maria A. Zayas. "Cardiac Coherence, Self-regulation, Autonomic Stability, and Psychosocial Well-being." Frontiers in Psychology 5 (2014). Accessed August 5, 2018. doi:10.3389/fpsyg.2014.01090.

7   Mccraty, Rollin, and Maria A. Zayas. "Cardiac Coherence, Self-regulation, Autonomic Stability, and Psychosocial Well-being." Frontiers in Psychology 5 (2014). Accessed August 5, 2018. doi:10.3389/fpsyg.2014.01090.

8   Mccraty, Rollin, and Maria A. Zayas. "Cardiac Coherence, Self-regulation, Autonomic Stability, and Psychosocial Well-being." Frontiers in Psychology 5 (2014). Accessed August 5, 2018. doi:10.3389/fpsyg.2014.01090.

9   Mccraty, Rollin, and Maria A. Zayas. "Cardiac Coherence, Self-regulation, Autonomic Stability, and Psychosocial Well-being." Frontiers in Psychology 5 (2014). Accessed August 5, 2018. doi:10.3389/fpsyg.2014.01090.

10   Dieterich-Hartwell, Rebekka. "Dance/movement Therapy in the Treatment of Post Traumatic Stress: A Reference Model." The Arts in Psychotherapy 54 (July 2017): 38-46. Accessed August 6, 2018. doi:10.1016/j.aip.2017.02.010.

11   Manitoba Trauma Information & Education Centre. "Taking Care of Your Spiritual Self." Trauma Recovery. http://trauma-recovery.ca/recovery/taking-care-of-your-spiritual-self/ (accessed August 6, 2018).

12   Merriam Webster Online, s.v. "Medicine." Accessed September 4, 2018, https://www.merriam-webster.com/dictionary/medicine.

13   Bandura, Albert. "Social Cognitive Theory: An Agentic Perspective." Annual Review of Psychology, 52 no 1 (2001) https://www.ebsco.com (accessed April 15, 2008).

14   Burger, Jerry. Personality. 7th ed. Belmont: Thomson Wadsworth, 2008.

15   Leichsenring, Falk, Wolfgang Hiller, Michael Weissberg, and Eric Leibing. "Cognitive-Behavioral Therapy and Psychodynamic Psychotherapy: Techniques, Efficacy, and Indications." American

Journal of Psychotherapy 60, no. 3 (2006): 233-59. doi:10.1176/appi.psychotherapy.2006.60.3.233

16 Corsini, Raymond and Danny Wedding. "Current Psychotherapies." 8th ed. Belmont: Thomson Brooks/Cole, 2008.

17 2 Cor. 10:5 NIV

18 Lk 22:42a NIV

19 Lk 22:42b NIV

20 Jer. 29:11 NIV

21 Wentzel, Kathryn and Allan Wigfield. *Handbook of Motivation at School*. New York: Routledge, 2009

22 Lk 23:46 NIV

23 Oxford Dictionaries, s.v. "routine," accessed September 4, 2018. https://en.oxforddictionaries.com/definition/routine

24 Goodreads. Accessed September 8, 2018,https://www.goodreads.com/quotes/871714-so-plant-your-own-gardens-and-decorate-your-own-soul

25 Acts 1:3 NIV

26 Acts 1:3 NIV

27 Isaiah 61:3 NIV

28 Mk 16:19 NIV

29 Goodreads. Accessed September 9, 2018, https://www.goodreads.com/quotes/460142-if-you-fail-to-plan-you-are-planning-to-fail

30 Hesselink, Gijs et al. "Improving Patient Discharge and Reducing Hospital Readmissions by Using Intervention Mapping." BMC Health Services Research 14, no. 1 (2014). Accessed September 9, 2018. doi:10.1186/1472-6963-14-389.

31 W. Clement Stone Quotes. BrainyQuote.com, Xplore Inc, 2018. https://www.brainyquote.com/quotes/w_clement_stone_193778, accessed September 9, 2018.

32 Thomas, Shannon. *Healing from Hidden Abuse*. Southlake: Mast Publishing, 2016.

CPSIA information can be obtained
at www.ICGtesting.com
Printed in the USA
FSHW021251140319
56374FS

9 781640 854536